Rethinking Learning To Read

By
Harriet Pattison

Forward by
Alan Thomas

Educational Heretics Press
www.educationalhereticspress.com

The right of Harriet Pattison to be identified as author of this work has been asserted by her in accordance with the Copyright, Designs and Patent Act, 1988.

Copyright © 2016 Harriet Pattison

Published 2016 by Educational Heretics Press
7 Cardington Drive, Shrewsbury, SY1 3HD
www.educationalhereticspress.com

British Cataloguing in Publication Data A CIP record for this book can be obtained from the British Library.

Pattison, Harriet
    Rethinking Learning To Read
    1. Home schooling – Great Britain 2. Home schooling – Research – Great Britain

ISBN: 978-1-900219-46-4

All rights reserved. No part of this publication may be reproduced, stored in a retrieval system, or transmitted in any form or by any means, electronic, mechanical, photocopying, recording or otherwise without the prior written permission of the publishers. This book may not be lent, hired out, resold or otherwise disposed of by way of trade in any form of binding or cover other than that in which it is published, without the prior consent of the publishers and without similar conditions being imposed on the subsequent purchasers.

The views expressed in this book are those of the individual authors, and do not necessarily represent the opinions of the editors or publishers.

Designed and typeset in Palatino Linotype by Educational Heretics Press
Cover design by Mike Wood
From original artwork: The Beauty of Nature © Haywiremedia
Supplied by agency: Dreamstime.com| ID 40435797

Printed and bound in Great Britain by
Imprint Digital, Seychelles Farm, Upton Pyne, Exeter, Devon EX5 5HY

For our children ...

Contents

Acknowledgements   9

Foreword: an historical introduction
- What written material was available   12
- Literacy rates   14
- Case study: Sweden   15
- How did they actually learn to read?   16
- The emergence of home education   18

Introduction   20

Chapter One   30
- Setting the home education Scene   30

Chapter Two   33
- Exploring understandings of learning   33
- What is learning and how can we go about understanding it?   33

Chapter Three   43
- What is reading?   43
- Understanding reading as a phonetic system   43
- Disagreeing with phonics   48
- Phonics and the individual   50
- Other Methods   52
- The limitations of method   52
- Methods that don't work   53
- No method   54
- Children devising their own method   55
- Memorising   56
- Silent reading   59
- Not knowing   62

Chapter Four   65
- To teach or not to teach? Structure vs autonomy   65
- Challenging teaching   66

What's different about teaching at home?	67
Individuality	68
Flexibility	69
Breaking up the teacher/learner relationship	71
Reading as cultural participation	73
Challenging the concept of teaching	77
Children's agency: resisting, requesting and doing it for yourself	80
Teaching being rejected	81
Requesting	83
Self-teaching	84
Pre-empting teaching	86
Moving from teaching to learning	87
Questioning the value of teaching	91

Chapter Five — 95

What do families do?	95
Reading aloud	95
Reading aloud as a form of transmission	95
Reading aloud as participation	98
What do children get out of being read to?	100
How often children are read to	103
Dynamic situations	104
Talking	105
Talk as a form of transmission	106
Answering children's questions	106
Talk as participation	109
Games/toys/computers	110
Children's play and other interests	113
Television	115

Chapter Six — 117

Learning trajectories	117
Reading trajectories	117
Standard reading trajectory	118
Downward curve learning	121
Downward curve	123
Non-progressive learning	124

What's happening in non-linear,
        non-progressive learning? 127

Chapter Seven 129

Assessment and 'late' reading 129
Assessment 129
How do you know when they are reading? 130
Demonstration 133
Observation 134
Questions 135
Children's own report 136
Late reading 138
The earlier, the better? 139

Chapter Eight 141

Expectations, pressure and child paced,
        child Led Philosophies of education 141
Social pressure 141
All children are different 145
Child paced, child led learning 147
Child paced 147
Child led learning 150
Challenging the role of reading and
        writing in education 152

Chapter Nine 155

Brothers and sisters and what happens in families 155
Explaining difference 156
Deficits within the child 156
Deficits within the environment 158

Chapter Ten 162

Coming out of school and special educational needs 162
Special educational needs 166
De-schooling 170

Chapter Eleven 175

Matters of motivation 175
The Role of motivation in learning to read 175

General motivation	177
Specific motivation	177
Which comes first…?	179

Chapter Twelve — 183

Considering learning to read through ideas of complexity	183
Constructing ideas about learning to read	183
Complexity	187
Complex self-organising systems	188
Applying the ideas of complexity to reading data	190
Possibilities rather than prescriptions	190
Dynamic systems	191
Organisation rather than accumulation	192
Metaphors of osmosis	192
Open systems	195
Continuing	196

Afterword	197
References	200
Index	207
About the Author	212

Acknowledgements

"All writing is ghost writing" ghost writes Mark Taylor (2001, p 196). What we write is never our own. Instead, the written word is a conduit through which flows a multitude of influences; thoughts, ideas and images gathered together, perhaps in unique confluences, but haunted always by multitudes of origins and projections which do not belong to their author and may indeed never be known to her. A book like this one perhaps stands even more closely than most to such a description, resting as it does on the insights, words and wisdom of the 311 parents who filled out the questionnaire on which this research is based and who shared their beliefs and their home educating worlds. For me, this research has been a meeting place, a space of shared thinking with like-minded people and a common quest to find understanding; to work together towards meanings that resonate in our own lives. It is clear that this book could not exist without these 311 contributors and clear also that through their combined contributions a unique conversation and testimony has been formed. I would like to thank each and every one for their co-authorship.

This research owes an enormous debt to Alan Thomas; indeed, without his inspiration, generosity and wisdom it would never have come about. Alan was instrumental and active in setting up this project and has remained a knowledgeable guide and critical friend throughout the years that have finally led to this publication. I am more than indebted to his experience, perception and understanding but his friendship has meant more to me than any of these things. He has not simply been a valued part of my work but a valued part of my life.

Also integral to the fruition of this work have been Mike Wood of Educational Heretics Press and Peter Humphreys of Personalised Education Now. It has been a breath of fresh air to escape the world of corporate publishing and work instead with passionate friends.

This book is based on my PhD research undertaken at the University of Birmingham under the supervision of Dr Nick Peim. I came home to the philosophical world he opened up to me and for that I am profoundly grateful. I would also like to thank my colleagues in the Department of Early Childhood at Liverpool Hope University. Their support has given me confidence and inspired me. I am very lucky to have them.

Finally, and of course, my beloved family who have indulged me so often and in so many ways and for so long.

This research has been part of my life for many years now and it will be strange to say goodbye. There have been highs, not many lows, a lot of fun and some thrilling moments of revelation in which I have felt as if I have glimpsed things beyond my own horizons. It seems more than fitting now to give thanks for such a wonderful opportunity and experience.

Foreword: an historical introduction
By Dr. Alan Thomas

To my knowledge, the research undertaken by Dr Harriet Pattison constitutes the first major study of how children learn to read outside an institutional setting. This is because, for nigh on 150 years, nearly all children have been taught to read in school. The popular belief is that prior to this, only a small minority of the population could read. Yet if we combine evidence from various historical sources we see a very different picture of children and adults increasingly becoming literate following the invention of printing in the fifteenth century. By the time schooling became more or less compulsory in 1876, at least two thirds of the population of England were already able to read.

> "In the absence of externally provided schools, indigenously supported settings were responsible for the creation and transmission of popular literacy. Thus over several centuries, the literate popular culture of England largely made itself." (Lacqueur, 1976, p.255)

From the early sixteenth century a great deal of written material became widely available including a surprisingly large amount of popular material aimed at the so called "lower orders" of society. What was actually available? How many adults and children were able to read? How did they learn to read?

Most people in the ruling classes, the church and certain professions had always been literate. Mass printing meant that written material became available to the masses for the first time. However, attempting to document the rise of literacy and especially how people became literate is fraught with difficulty. The reason is that, until the nineteenth century hardly anyone was interested in the lives of the lower orders and did not expect (or want) them to be able to read.

> "For the last thousand years or more at least 70% and sometimes as many as 90% of the population have been ordinary (common) people who had to work to make a living and were ruled by a small minority who lived off the labour of the majority... When the common people appear in history at all they are not central but only in the background, almost like characters off-stage". (Harrison, 1988, p.17)

Given the rapid growth of written material widely available, it would have been very difficult for most people not to become acquainted with it whether through learning to read or at the very least being read to by someone of equal status who was literate. That they did so is underlined by the steady increase in literacy rates throughout the period prior to schooling. Where there was a compelling motivation for everyone to learn to read, as in Sweden, almost the whole population became literate in a very short period of time, despite the almost total lack of schooling.

What written material was available

Following the invention of printing in the fifteenth century, a wide range of written material became increasingly available. Most obviously, the Bible was translated into English and printed though there was tremendous resistance from the Church to ordinary people even hearing it their own tongue let alone reading it. Because of this it was not until much later that it became common for people to have a copy in their own homes.

At the same time, the commercial opportunity offered by

mass publishing for a wide audience did not go unnoticed and led to the proliferation of written material in various forms. "Broadsides" were single sheets of paper which carried such things as proclamations, news and ballads. Almanacs were published throughout the period right up to modern times. Ballads were also very popular. As early as the 1520s an Oxford bookseller, John Dorne, recorded selling up to 190 ballads a day at a halfpenny each.

Most important of all were the popular and cheap "chapbooks." These were usually single sheets folded into "books" of a small number of pages. They first appeared from the early sixteenth and lasted well into the nineteenth century. They were sold all around England, door to door, at markets and fairs. For the most part, chapbooks catered to popular interests: love, war, the supernatural and highly coloured historical narratives. They were cheap and generally affordable to nearly everyone, read in homes and alehouses. The numbers printed are astonishing. One 17th-century publisher of chapbooks in London had in stock one chapbook for every 15 families in the country. In the 1660s as many as 400,000 almanacs were printed annually, enough for one family in three in England. By the end of the eighteenth century, when Thomas Paine's "The Rights of Man" was published it immediately sold nearly a million copies. Popular newspapers also appeared around this time, catering for increasing demands for entertainment and sensational news.

Religious publications also became widely available, especially following the publication of the King James version of the Bible in 1611. Tradition has it that nearly all households would have owned a Bible, often in which would be written family names and events. Other publications in common ownership were The Book of

Common Prayer and The Catechism. The Pilgrim's Progress, first published in 1678 was reprinted 160 times up to 1792, aside from other pirated editions.

Literacy rates

Given the sheer amount and variety of written material, both religious and popular, it is almost inconceivable that a substantial proportion of the population would not have learned to read. Actually establishing how many could read is another matter.

In England, the main indicator of literacy in the working class used by historians is the ability to sign one's name on official documents, at weddings for example. Those who could not sign simply provided a mark. On the surface it appears reasonable to conclude that those who could sign would be literate. It's also possible that they learned to sign their names without being able to read. After all, many very young children can write their names long before they can read. Also, those who were able to read might not have been able to write and were therefore timid about attempting to sign their names and so just left their mark. Others might have followed the expectation that they should not be able to read, there being a widespread fear among the ruling classes that a literate peasantry might get access to radical political publications or ideas above their station.

Such evidence as there is points to steadily increasing literacy rates in England from the early sixteenth century. It is generally thought that male literacy rose from around 30% in the seventeenth century to 60% by the mid-eighteenth century. Female literacy rates also improved but at a lesser rate - women were not encouraged to learn to read or possibly were reluctant to admit that they could.

It is commonly supposed that literacy increased dramatically with the introduction of universal schooling. Yet by this time at least three quarters of the population were already literate.

> "Historians have generally assumed that literacy increased dramatically with the introduction of universal schooling in 1876 when most of the populace was literate anyway... Schooling came to make a difference when that part of the population, 65% to 75% who could become literate through traditional cultural processes had become so. It was for the residual 25% or so... that schools were more relevant. These are the people reflected in the data on the very rapid decline in illiteracy during the last half of the nineteenth century." (Lacquer, op cit, 269)

Case study: Sweden

The growth of literacy in Sweden illustrates how children learnt to read with little if any formal instruction, from 35% literate in 1760 to 90% by 1820 at a time when almost the entire population consisted of agrarian peasantry. It had nothing to do with industrialisation, so how did it come about?

With regard to evidence, what is striking is that figures are based on an entire population. Internationally, most social historians have had to be content with estimates based on very little data, such as the ability to sign one's name. But in Sweden, a pastor and social historian, Egil Johansson, discovered virtually complete data for an entire population, updated annually and running for centuries. The motivation to learn to read is clear. Following a royal directive, any person unable to read was not allowed to take holy communion and therefore could not marry. (Graff et al

2009).

The ability to read was vigorously tested. Johansson had discovered records kept by...

> "... Lutheran pastors on the reading and comprehension abilities of all their parishioners, household by household, from cradle to grave. Babies, children, servants, those passing through, and the elderly, however old, were all included by royal proclamation. From roughly the 1640s to the early twentieth century, these records were... more or less intact for the country as a whole and its far-flung empire in the seventeenth century. Even the Swedish American colony and immigrants arriving in Delaware, Illinois, and Minnesota since the 1850s were not exempt from the church examination register process" (Graff et al, 2009, p.8).

What the Swedish example tells us is that virtually anyone can become literate given the motivation and availability of reading material. In England it might not have been imperative to learn to read and there was undoubtedly antagonism to the masses becoming literate. However, apart from religious motivation to read the Bible and other religious texts, there were many impetuses to learn to read; for economic purposes, for self-improvement, to gain access to radical political ideas or simply because the more popular publications offered entertainment, gossip and sensational news.

How did they actually learn to read?

How people learnt to read throughout history is almost impossible to establish. It is obvious that they would not have learnt formally, certainly not in the school sense although this has somehow become accepted by the large majority to be the only method.

> "Since the Second World War the accepted model has been to regard it as necessary that... formal school instruction should be almost the only conceivable teaching method... A general ability to read in a poor, pre-industrial, agrarian, developing country like Sweden or Finland seems a sheer absurdity" (Graff et al, p. 31).

With regard to how they learnt, there is so little to go on, even in Sweden. Once they could read, they could read. The processes that they went through in order to do so are clouded in mystery. There are only a few clues. As a Scottish visitor to Sweden noted:

> "The parents were the teachers of their children, till they reached the age of fourteen or thereabouts, when they attended the pastor or his assistant, to be prepared for confirmation and being admitted to the Lord's Supper" (Graff et al, 2009, p.29).

This does not take us very far. Similarly, in England, there are only tantalising glimpses into how lower class people became literate. Attempting to explain the growth of literacy from the sixteenth century Laquer (1976) suggests that...

> "Smatterings of these skills might be acquired as the opportunity and necessity arose so that the process was organically related to the rest of life" (p.259).

Harrison (1988) while acknowledging that informal schools might have played a part, many children "learned to read and sometimes to write, from their parents, friends or neighbours, in various informal settings and at times convenient to other tasks" (p. 228).

While there was no compunction to learn to read in England, the majority of people still did so. It was generally not for economic or occupational demands. It is far more likely that they learned in smatterings, informally, over an extended period of time. There were also those whose families sought self-improvement or wished their children to read the scriptures in which case they might have set out deliberately to teach them to read.

An interesting possibility concerns the likely role of religious reading matter. Nearly all children would have been familiar with certain sections of the Bible, with the catechism and prayer book, parts of which they would have known by heart. It is difficult not to imagine that curiosity would not have led many to become acquainted with the written word in this way.

And that is about as far as we get. However, we do now have the opportunity to learn more about informal processes of learning to read though the experience of home educating families. It's true that today both motivation and opportunity to learn to read have grown dramatically and opportunities for engaging with the written word abound in a way almost unimaginable for our ancestors. That they did so throughout history is a tribute to their ingenuity and tenacity.

The emergence of home education

From 1876 to the present it has been widely accepted that children will not learn to read unless they are directly and formally taught, so much so that until relatively recently parents were actively discouraged from teaching their children to read because it would interfere with professional expertise and methodology. Even today, parental help is viewed only in terms of general support and not teaching.

It was not until home education became more prevalent that

it was feasible to return to the question of learning to read outside formal institutions. An early and iconic example is provided by Joy Baker's children who learned to read informally. She decided to educate her children at home in the early 1950s and was forced into a battle through the courts which lasted for 10 years from 1952 until 1962 when she finally obtained a judgement in her favour. She was a genuine pioneer who challenged both the educational and legal establishment at the time. Here she describes to the court how her children learnt to read, echoing the experiences of all those children and adults who learned to read throughout the centuries.

> "None of my children have been taught to read. They have always been given suitable reading matter... I have found that under these circumstances they learn to read slowly but far more efficiently than a great many children formally taught at the expense of many wasted hours at a school desk... I am told that my children are backward because they learned to read later than the accepted standard but they have never so far suffered any disadvantage from this" (Baker, 1964 p.124)

To sum up, how very many children and adults learned to read throughout history, with little or no direct tuition or method, confronts the existing educational doctrine that children will not learn to read unless their learning is planned systematically step by step. As Dr Pattison describes in the following pages, the way that individual children get to grips with the printed word varies enormously and is in direct opposition to school practice of teaching all children to read at the same age and by the same method.

Introduction

"Reading, like language coalesces out of the mist"

Home educating parent

This book is about how children learn to read. A great deal of research has been devoted to this subject, perhaps more than to any other area of education. Becoming literate is of paramount importance in the modern world; a matter that may not be left to chance but which requires the thoughtful, early and systematic intervention of the agents of education. In our society the "concerted cultivation" of literacy is a predominant interest for schools, policy makers and families alike (Prins and Toso, 2008, p 565). Instruction and the monitored development of pre-reading skills begins formally in the UK at the age of four and is statutory within the Early Years Foundation Stage (Department for Education, 2012). By the time children are entering compulsory education at five reading has become central to most of their lives. Certainly its place in schooling is pivotal. It seems that few would disagree with Stainthorp and Hughes when they say that "one of the most important tasks, if not *the* most important task of the early-years' teacher is to teach children to read and write" (Stainthorp and Hughes, 1999, p 1, italics in original).

There are good reasons behind the drive to get children reading early and efficiently in their school careers. Formal schooling relies critically on a child's ability to read and write and without the normative skill level in these areas children suffer across the curriculum. The outlook for those unable to make the grade in the early stages becomes increasingly bleak as they progress through the primary years. Those who are still not reading at a satisfactory level on transferring from primary to secondary school are unlikely ever to recover (Slavin, Lake, Davis and Madden 2009). The consequences of poor reading stretch through the school years, seriously impacting on exam results, and continue into depressed prospects in the world beyond compulsory education. Teaching reading has therefore become a priority for schools and educational policy and a cause of anxiety for parents, teachers and children alike. Fischer (2003) reports myriad practices for, and theories on, the teaching of reading across the past two centuries and the production of modern schemes and advice continues apace. Synthetic phonics is the much championed flavour of the moment but has competition from other methods such as 'look and say' as well as the accompaniment of a vast research literature on the importance of the 'correct' literacy home background.

Given this cultural and educational context, this book is about an unusual group of people. Characterising them is not easy; but they are all home educators who have, in one way or another, questioned and confronted the prevailing procedures and practices of learning to read. The practices of these families and their attitudes towards, and philosophies of, reading, frequently vary from the main stream and in some cases contradict conventional thought altogether.

In one of the first studies of home education practices Alan Thomas (1998) found the acquisition of literacy emerging as a major theme of his research. Parents teaching their children to read at home used a variety of methods even within the same family, and children's own interests and preferred time scales were considered to be an important, if not the deciding factor in how and when reading instruction took place. For other families, instruction seemed to play little or no part with parents describing how their children had simply begun reading although no one could explain how this had come about. Of equal interest from this study was the revelation that the age at which children learned to read, so critical in school, was apparently of little or no consequence at home. Many children learned 'late' by school standards but there was no discernible knock on effect and learning in other areas appeared unaffected. In this sample of 100 families, a significant number of children began reading after the age of 7 (generally considered the school norm for fluent reading) and up to the age of 10. These children often seemed to progress very quickly once they started reading and to achieve age related standards or above within a matter of months.

In our follow up research, (Thomas and Pattison 2007,) we concentrated on informal learning amongst home educated children and again returned to the matter of literacy. In this sample of 77 children some children were reported as not reading up to the age of 12 and for others it seemed that although they might be able to read there was no desire to do so until well into their teens. Parents were willing guides for their children's explorations of literacy and many reported reading unlimited amounts aloud for their children's entertainment. All seemed to offer the kind of literate home background believed to be vital in fostering learning to read. Yet the responses from the children were mixed with some rejecting outright the idea of reading for themselves and resisting any attempts to be taught no matter how individualised or gentle the proffered tuition. Instead, parents talked about the role of hobbies and leisure activities which required reading at some point or about their child's desire to read a particular story or to investigate a particular interest and how such incentives could become the turning point which led into literacy. We speculated on the influence of living in a literate environment, not just at the level of the family, but at the level of society as well and how knowledge and understanding about reading might simply be absorbed over long years of undirected exposure to the written word that surrounds us in our everyday lives. We attempted to see learning to read as something specifically embedded in other experiences, the need to follow computer prompts or to play card games for example. We considered again how the difference in time scales between the expectations held of children in school and the considerably lesser pressure on home educated children might allow learning to read at home to be a radically different experience. Nevertheless, the feeling persisted that the heart of the matter was continuing to elude us.

There is little available in current research literature to help further our understanding here. Reading research is overwhelmingly concentrated on the experiences of children in school and although there is an important body of socio-cultural work that looks at children's out of school literacy practices and experiences it is impossible to separate what the effects of this might be from the teaching which children routinely receive in school. Although there appears to be widespread anecdotal evidence that it is not unusual for children to 'pick up' reading before they begin school, there have been only two studies of this phenomenon to date. Margaret Clark in 1976 carried out a study of 32 Scottish children who had learned to read prior to starting school, whilst in 1999 Rhona Stainthorp and Diana Hughes published the results of a three-year study which followed a group of children who had learned to read without being taught from pre-school to the end of Year 2. Helpful though both of these studies have been in contributing to the thinking in this book they are not able to answer the questions posed by the home educating families' experiences. A string of puzzles surrounding both these texts, as well as Alan Thomas' and our joint research, remained without satisfactory answers. How were these children learning to read? Where were the cause and effect links that would let us understand their experiences? What made these children's experiences different from each other and where were the common threads? Is there a kind of teaching so subtle that it goes unnoticed? What is it that a person is actually doing when they are reading? This book is the result of attempts to return to these and other questions and, using the evidence, thoughts and words of home educating families, to rethink what it means to learn to read.

The data on which this book is based was gathered using a website questionnaire which Alan Thomas and I set up jointly in 2009. We invited home educating parents to respond to 11 questions about how their child had learned to read; stressing that we were interested in all manner of experiences and approaches and wanting to hear their stories whether good or bad. In all we received 311completed questionnaires, some from parents responding about an individual child, some from parents who told us about multiple children. In all, the questionnaires covered 215 boys and 184 girls and one child for whom no sex was given. This makes a total of 400 children. Two adults who had been home educated themselves also responded. Not all the children were described as 'readers' by their parents but all had recognisable literary lives. The children termed readers had learned to read anywhere between the ages of 18 months and 16 years old. A wide range of approaches and ideas about learning and reading were represented, providing me with much food for thought as I analysed the responses and attempted to rethink learning to read through the rich and fascinating stories which parents detailed. It has been an enormous privilege to work with such strong and insightful data and I hope to have done justice to the effort and thought with which parents responded. For ease of reference each contributing adult has been allocated a number followed by either M or F (referring to the sex of the child) or the letters Fam indicating that they were responding about more than one child.

Potential respondents were alerted to the existence of the questionnaire through a notice in the [1]Education Otherwise (EO) UK bi-monthly newsletter, through key contacts, word of mouth and announcement at a major home education event (HESFES) in the UK. The website address was also published at the end of some articles written at the time for 'Juno' (a natural parenting magazine) and for 'Who Cares?' which is the newsletter of the organisation Full Time Mothers. Links to the website were also posted on the EO and [2]School house websites. The aim behind the

---

[1] Education Otherwise advertises itself as "a membership organisation providing support and information for families whose children are educated outside school and for those who wish to uphold the freedom of families to take proper responsibility for the education of their children." It operates UK wide.

[2] Schoolhouse advertises itself as an organisation which "offers information and support to parents and carers throughout Scotland who seek to take personal responsibility for the education of their children". It operates in Scotland.

advertising was to gain as large a sample as possible although there was no provision for people who might have wanted to respond but were without access to the internet. In fact, enthusiasm for the questionnaire became quite widespread and unsolicited publicity in the USA and Australia led to an unforeseen rate of response from abroad. Responses were also received from New Zealand and mainland Europe.

The number of returns was very pleasing but quantity was not their only merit. The depth of thinking, the insight and perception of the returns was remarkable. It was clear that many people shared a deep interest in reading and were thinking hard about their experiences and seeking new ways to understand learning in general and learning to read in particular. It was also clear that people wanted to talk about these things and were keen to share their experiences. Part of this may be attributable to the political environment of 2009 - 10 when data was being collected. Home educators in the UK were confronting the Badman Review and it seemed that much of the freedom which had surrounded home education in the UK was to be lost. Perhaps there was a feeling that an urgent record was needed or perhaps that research could help explain and justify the practices of home education to those who found them strange or even dangerous. Many responses came from other countries however and were unlikely to have had such a pressing political edge, yet much that was contained in the Badman Review went beyond the direct action recommended to the UK government and into the educational discourse and views that prevail in other modern, Western societies. It is this discourse which this research aims to re-think so that something as commonplace and ordinary as learning to read, accomplished by millions of children across the world, can be made strange again, re-thought, in the space which home education provides.

The responses were wide ranging and included many shades of home educators: religiously motivated, radical unschoolers, families following structured programmes, autonomous learners, children who had spent some time in school and those who had never been. Advocates of phonics and many other approaches to reading were represented. Despite this diversity however, this is not a random sample nor one from which it is possible to generalise about either home education or reading.

Criticisms of sampling have bedevilled home education research and are frequently the cited reason for dismissing the findings of such research. For example, the Badman Review of 2009 rejected the relevance of small sample research arguing that low numbers of self-selected accounts were not sufficient grounds from which to make decisions about the majority (Badman, 2009). Although the current sample of 311 families constitutes a substantial cohort it makes no claim to being representative. Indeed, because there is no reliable secondary data on home education in the UK and because accurate numbers or any kind of demographic profile of home educators are unknown (Petrie, Windrass and Thomas 1998) any sample to population generalisation is impossible. There is simply not enough information available to claim that any cohort of home educators can be seen as representative of a wider population. Even if more were known about the home educating population, a sample to population generalisation would still not constitute valid educational thinking. In what ways the sample represented the whole would depend on the variables considered pertinent and these in themselves would constitute a theory of learning. A further discussion of the methodological details pertaining to this study are presented in Pattison (2014).

However, none of these difficulties mean that inquiry is impossible nor that such work should not be taken seriously. Research such as that presented here is able to offer a qualitative and exploratory account through which to challenge assumptions and offer new insights. Sample limitations do not interfere with this; the aim being to concentrate on the understandings which can be found from within the sample and to begin critically examining how learning at home takes place rather than to ascertain the prevalence of such practices or to link any other characteristics with home education or its forms.

It is also possible to take up the idea of what Robert Stake calls "naturalistic generalisation" (Stake, 2000, p23). This kind of generalisation is not to do with the formal matching procedures of research but arises as people share information and ideas and in doing so see similarities between their own experiences and those of others. Accounts of children learning to read circulate through home educating communities, newsletters and web site forums, publications and home education gatherings. Parents are able to combine this community knowledge and experience with their own personal, situational knowledge to make individual choices about their children's education, thus generalising on a personal and often instinctive level. This work may well resonate with some in similar ways.

However, this book is not intended as a guide of the 'how to' kind and it offers parents no suggestions about how they should or should not approach either literacy in particular or home education in general. Instead it is concerned with analysing the experiences of the home educating families and reflecting philosophically upon them. The French philosophers and political activists Gilles Deleuze and Felix Guattari (1987) put forward a view of research as a map rather than a tracing of the subject matter under investigation. Using this comparison, we might make the analogy of using a satellite navigation system vs a map to traverse London. The sat nav tells you when to turn and how far to go before you turn again; against the idea of a map which makes numerous routes possible without any suggestions itself about which might be best or right or even the one most frequently taken. This research seeks to be a map about the possibilities that surround learning to read; not about what should happen or even about what does happen. This may seem a little strange compared to the overwhelming thrust of educational research that is concerned with best practice, raising standards, improving outcomes and guaranteeing results. Such research is couched in terms of the sat nav that tells you what to do and how to do it in order to progress from A to B. By contrast this book is an exploratory map, a return to the rough ground and as such an opportunity to genuinely rethink learning to read. In doing so I am ever mindful that all understanding, including the attempts here, offer only temporally and contextually specific points of view. That we recognise all knowledge as perception in no way detracts from its meaningfulness, neither from its ability to cast light on our assumptions and I offer the following exploration in this spirit.

Chapter One begins with a brief overview of home education; its growth over recent years and the opportunity which this offers to educational research and thinking. Chapter Two examines the concept of learning and looks particularly at how the use of metaphor affects the ways in which we understand learning and how such metaphors, in turn, inform our educational decisions. In Chapter Three I examine how we understand reading, this time rooting the discussion in the understandings of reading brought forward by home educators. Chapter Four offers an exploration of issues surrounding teaching and learning and considers how the home educating families challenge the common connections made between these two aspects of education. Chapter Five explores the part which families felt they had played in their children's learning and includes discussions of the influence of reading aloud, talking, playing games and watching TV. Learning trajectories and the different paths which learning can take for different children is the subject of Chapter Six. Chapter Seven considers issues of assessing reading and the designation of 'late' reading and this theme is continued in Chapter Eight in which social and educational pressure is discussed, particularly in the light of the child led and child paced learning philosophies to which many home educating parents aspire. Chapter Nine looks more closely into individual differences in how and when children learn to read by considering the differences between siblings of the same family. Chapter Ten concentrates on children who are taken out of school where reading forms part of that decision and also looks at designations of Special Educational Needs and the accounts of families where this has been an additional consideration. Chapter

Eleven looks at how motivation affects learning to read and what happens in cases where children seem to entirely lack motivation. Chapter Twelve, the final chapter, considers understanding reading through the ideas of complexity. Finally, a short afterword argues the importance of how we understand learning to read as not just an educational matter but an ethical one as well.

Chapter One

Setting the home education Scene

Home education is a movement which, from small beginnings, is now gathering global momentum (Global Home Education Conference, 2012). Its growth is an unprecedented phenomenon in the field of education not just in terms of its spread and participation but also in terms of the disturbance of ideas it brings to a world in which education has become all but synonymous with schooling (Suissa, 2006). New practices, philosophies and understandings of education are, with the rise of home education, becoming real possibilities for both praxis and thinking.

Home education is a legal option in most western countries (exceptions being Germany and Sweden) although legal requirements, including the registration of children who do not attend school, vary from country to country (Rothermel, 2015). In the UK the extent to which the option of home education is exercised is a matter of speculation as no official statistics are kept. There is no legal compulsion to register a home educated child with the local authority if that child has never attended school, nor is there a legal compulsion to inform the new local authority if a child not attending school moves residence from one local authority area to another (Nicholson, 2012). Reliable information is therefore very difficult to collect. What began as a handful of families in the 1970s (Meighan, 1997) had grown to estimates of between 50,000 and 70,000 children in 2009 (Fortune-Wood, 2009). It will now never be possible to chart the rise of home education in the UK; what does seem certain though is that numbers are growing rapidly – perhaps by as much as 15 per cent per annum (Fortune-Wood, 2009). It is a trend which all the available indications suggest to be an international one; the United States Department of Education put the 2012 figure of children being educated at home at 1.7 million or 3.4% of the school population (US Department of Education, 2012).

Not only are numbers in the UK unknown but so is the detail of how parents go about educating their children at home. Home educating families are not obliged to follow the national curriculum, take GCSEs or standard tests, make advance plans or keep school hours, terms or timetables. Nor are they restrained by any of the physical or policy restrictions that govern the possibilities for teachers and classes in most mainstream schools. The result is that home educators are free to follow their own ideologies, design their own practices and come to their own conclusions about the possibilities and purposes of the educational enterprise (see for example Dowty, 2000).

From research, personal testimonies, anecdotal evidence, newsletters and submitted evidence in court cases it is clear that home educators span a range of ideas and positions. Despite being lumped together by legislation, the media and even occasionally themselves, there is no such thing as a typical home educator. Thomas (1998) interviewed 100 home educating families revealing a broad spectrum of approaches to, and ideas about, education, from 'more like school than school' through to very informal approaches that seemed to hold little if anything in common with mainstream descriptions of education. One phenomenon that did emerge from the data was that families tended to drift towards the informal even if they had begun home educating formally with lessons, curriculum and timetable. As Thomas puts it, "virtually all the parents ... found themselves moving towards less structure and greater informality" (Thomas, 1998, p 53). Of these, some came to believe that education without any formal input was a real possibility and "just a few put this belief into practice" (Thomas, 1998, p 54). Such a form of education Thomas sees as more than a flexible approach to learning; rather these parents have discovered a "genuine alternative to structured education of the kind experienced by children in school" (Thomas, 1998, p 53).

The drift towards and the practice of such informal education is important because philosophically it also represents a drift away from the dominant understandings that govern our ideas about what happens in school; indeed, such a drift has potentially an even bigger portent. In our society school is more than the mental, physical, emotional, social and intellectual environment of childhood; it is a world orientation that encompasses a whole theory of mind (Bruner, 1996); a practical, cultural definition of how human beings work. Given the totality of the school experience, it is not surprising that amongst the population of children who do not go to school and amongst their families there are different ideas emerging and circulating about how human beings work. That is not to say that all home educators agree, nor to say that families where children do go to school might not share some of these views, nor to deny that the long arm of education extends its influence well beyond the school gate. Only to say, that the new landscape of home education allows different practices, different ideas, different desires about education to surface and that embedded in these may be different understandings of what it means to be a thinking, learning human being. The home educating families' accounts and experiences of learning to read offer a rich opportunity to explore the possibilities of such understandings.

Chapter Two

Exploring understandings of learning

To rethink learning to read necessitates a closer look at our fundamental understandings of the two main concepts to be drawn on: learning and reading. In this chapter I begin attempting to unravel how we comprehend these ideas and to consider how our perceptions of both reading and learning create the particular conceptual synthesis by which we understand learning to read.

What is learning and how can we go about understanding it?

Learning, like love and freedom, is an abstract concept. We cannot examine it through empirical evidence; we cannot touch, smell, or observe it. Instead we can only infer it by watching for clues and assuming those clues to be signs that somehow reveal learning to us; in the same way that a gesture might reveal love, although it is not itself love. The offering of an engagement ring for example, is not love but would generally be taken as a sign of love. As far as learning is concerned the clues we might look for could be changes to behaviour, activities, speech and character and in seeing alterations in these things, at least in so far as they are deemed positive, we tend to argue that they reveal learning. So if Sam can read some words this week that he struggled over last we say he has learned; the reading of the few more words is the sign that reveals learning.

We infer learning through signs that appear to indicate learning but these clues must themselves rest on an understanding of what learning is. Otherwise how do we know how to understand them? Why should they be signs of learning and not signs of something else? Why should they be signs at all? In the tangible engagement ring we see a host of allusions to the abstractions of commitment, fidelity, and future; ideas which connect to our theories of love and which are further sustained through deep cultural attachments to the importance of these things as well as the further practices that surround them. The same pattern of meaning making occurs when we think about learning. When Sam reads the few extra words our conviction that he has learned can be very hard to repress. Yet our recognition of this behaviour as a sign of learning is inevitably linked to our cultural understandings of what learning is and its importance. We take the behaviour as a representation of something we cannot explicitly see. So his extra words allude in the observer's mind to ideas about understanding, progressing, developing, demonstrating, that underlie our theories of learning. To see the distinction here it may be helpful to think about debates in which it is sometimes argued that if a child has memorised words this is not the same as learning to read. The sign, which is a child reciting words from a text, can be understood as learning or memorising, reading or not reading, depending on the theory behind the interpretation. Without such a theory we cannot explain the significance of saying the extra words.

As an abstract concept we need to approach learning through theorisation, by attaching an interpretation to behaviour and this in turn we do through culturally defined ideas about learning. That this is so is regularly obscured through the cultural shorthand which turns signs into meaning in ways which conceal that interpretation has ever taken place. The waters of construal can be muddied yet further by the addition of symbols to the melee. If the reading of the few more words is the sign of learning, then the gold star sticker is the symbol that objectifies the sign. Inferences have become tangible objects in such a smooth and familiar flow that it can be hard to notice this has even happened. Furthermore, the symbol itself can become an object of worth and emotion; symbols have meanings which are very real to us and have a very real impact on our lives. The child who has just been given her gold star knows she has learned, knows she is clever and feels proud – all things which she understands through the symbolic significance of the little bit of coloured paper. As I. M. Lewis puts it, "Symbols possess both intellectual and emotional (or affectual) efficacy" (Lewis, 1985, p 110).

Symbols become incredibly important in how we go about understanding the world, how we behave in it and how we feel and education is a symbol rich field. Education is considered in our society to be a valued ideal and one in which learning is judged as central. So learning is good, important and worthy of symbolic representation. Our common symbols of learning range from gold stars to grades, certificates to letters after our names and whilst the connection between symbol and learning, once stripped down, is recognisably crude the worth of the symbol is no less denied by the inadequacies of the connection. So a child who gets ten out of ten is cleverer than a child who gets three out of ten; a person with a degree is more knowledgeable than a person without one, the teenager with a clutch of GCSEs is more capable than the teenager with none. This is so to the point that, our society's confusion between the symbol and the thing it symbolises is perhaps the greatest entrenched illusion of the western education system (Peim and Flint, 2009). Certainly in the UK the political scramble to claim the symbols of education (more children with GCSE passes) has all but overwhelmed education. The result is that a powerful symbolic system based on evidence which emanates tautologically from its own structure of representation has become the dominant discourse of education in our institutions and society.

If we want to re-think learning we have to think away from, or at least raise awareness of, the symbolic system by which it is represented. Part of this entails thinking our way out of symbolic structures like school grades. But far more challenging even than this is thinking our way out of the symbolic system of language which governs our understanding of learning. In an oft quoted phrase the philosopher Ludwig Wittgenstein argues that "philosophy is a battle against the bewitchment of our intelligence by means of language" (Wittgenstein, 1953, p 109). We have a powerful discourse (language, vocabulary, concepts) surrounding learning which works to control not only how we talk about education but which also governs how we think about learning. Learning, we have said, is an abstract concept and how we approach the abstract in any field of knowledge is a complicated issue. At the heart of the matter lies the problem of how to handle ideas which take us beyond our empirical senses. A possible answer to this question, which this book takes as one of its main themes of exploration, was proposed by Michael Reddy in 1978. In a highly influential academic paper he argued that our understanding of the abstract is made possible through the use of metaphor.

Most of us understand metaphors in a literary sense, thinking of English language classes in which similes and metaphors are hunted out from poems and prose as stylistic embellishments. Following Reddy's paper however, many scholars have taken up the idea of metaphor as playing a fundamental role in how we think, how we understand the non-empirical and how we use and are comfortable with difficult concepts such as love and learning. These scholars argue that metaphor is not just in our language but is deeply embedded in our understanding; forming in fact its basis. Metaphors are the means that allow us to address the abstract concepts through which our thinking and understanding of the world occurs (Lakoff and Johnson, 1980). Metaphors work by likening concepts to empirical subject matter, they allow us to visualise things we cannot see. They make connections between the tangible and the abstract; the world of our senses and the world of our thought. The poet can use these connections to paint startlingly vivid depictions of deep felt emotions, like the black pit that illustrates despair but equally on a more practical level we might liken brain function to a computer or communication to a flow.

Metaphors, argues Anna Sfard, are not just the stuff of the layman's thinking; she considers that metaphors "underlie both our spontaneous everyday conceptions and scientific theorizing" (Sfard, 1998, p 4), including our thinking about learning. Indeed, R. K. Elliot argues that in educational thought metaphors are not just helpful but essential; "theories of learning are dependent on metaphors, because they are centrally concerned either with mental acts and conscious processes or with the operations of mental mechanisms below the level of consciousness, all of which are describable only by metaphorical means" (Elliot, 1984, p 38). The use of metaphor in educational literature and discourse is widespread and influential; structuring our understanding in subtle and not so subtle ways. Yet we tend not to notice their existence let alone the powerful influence they wield (Holt, 1984). Indeed, so embedded is the use of metaphor that it is more than a way of understanding but also the basis on which we rationalise choices and defend or enact particular educational practices. Because of this our adoption of a particular metaphor is not to be taken lightly; as Sfard puts it, the "choice of a metaphor is a highly consequential decision. Different metaphors may lead to different ways of thinking" (Sfard, 1998, p5) which in turn will alter how we view and conduct the whole enterprise of education.

According to Sfard (1998) education is caught between two metaphors - that of acquisition and that of participation. She goes on to argue that metaphors which liken learning to an acquisition use the idea of the human mind as a container to be filled with knowledge. This knowledge then becomes the personal possession of its owner. Learning is about gaining ownership of knowledge (although the same argument may be used about the acquisition of skill); a personal, mental accumulation. Such a metaphorical understanding is marked by the use of vocabulary such as grasping, retaining, internalising, cramming to characterise the act of learning whilst the role of the teacher is to transmit, deliver, or convey subject matter to the mind of the learner (Sfard, 1998).

Learning as the acquisition of knowledge leads to the further metaphorical idea of constructing knowledge. Knowledge can be gained bit by bit, each new acquisition joining the bits already assembled in layers like building blocks. Thus the metaphor now becomes a process; knowledge is acquired piece by piece so that learning is akin to a progressive construction that we often argue will lead, in a further expansion of the metaphor, to 'higher levels' of knowledge or understanding. We can argue that this kind of picture is just a visual short hand for something over which we still have very little comprehension but we need also to be wary; once these ideas are established they become instrumental guiding forces that embody a logic of their own. A flick through the Department for Education's 'Reading the Next Steps' (2015) shows a peppering of such metaphors including 'building' 'attaining', 'grasping', 'mastering' and 'acquiring'. In fact, this document is illustrative of our most common understanding of reading as an object of learning; reading is both implicitly and explicitly characterised as being the personal acquisition of a bundle of pertinent knowledge which will re-emerge demonstrably as a standardised skill. Such metaphors create very authoritative pictures of what it means to learn; pictures which are so engrained in our thinking that they can be incredibly hard even to question. Because of them it seems natural for us to recourse to the idea that reading is a cognitive skill; something which happens within the heads of individuals and this through a process of personal acquisition of exclusive skills which then become private possessions.

The wide spread use of metaphors of acquisition, as indicated above, is commonplace and was similarly echoed in many of the home educators' questionnaire responses. A handful serve to illustrate:

> 3M: "He acquired the skills
>
> 29Fam: "As long as you give them the tools …"
>
> 78M: "Once he had the basics, he did the rest himself"
>
> 76M: "He went from having a grasp of simple phonetic words …"
>
> 72M: "he just absorbed the skills himself …"

Sfard's second metaphor of education is that of participation. The great shift here she argues is that of replacing 'having' with 'doing'. Whilst acquisition centres on private possession, participation suggests group endeavour; whilst acquisition points to a finite good, participation is to do with on-going activity. In participation individual action and context are inextricably linked – we cannot participate unless we are participating in something. The kind of vocabulary employed in these metaphors is therefore about situation, context, cultural embeddedness, contribution and involvement and the aim of learning is to become a member of a community rather than to acquire personal knowledge. The learner is a member of a group whose interests lie in participating with other members of the group rather than in the pursuit of individual ends and gain; "learning a subject is now conceived of as a process of becoming a member of a certain community. This entails, above all, the ability to communicate in the language of this community and act according to its particular norms" (Sfard, 1998, p4). Such learning is perhaps best exemplified in theories of apprenticeship such as those of Rogoff (1990) or Lave and Wenger (1991) both of which will be fully discussed in later chapters. As well as using the more common acquisition metaphors parents' comments frequently lent themselves to an interpretation resting on ideas of participation as the following quotes illustrate:

> 38Fam: "Everyone else was doing it, they wanted to do it too."
>
> 57F: "Observing others reading, having a desire to do the same has been the biggest motivator."
>
> 16F: "If they are surrounded by it they will want to do it."

Although reading is rarely addressed through such a metaphor (Frank Smith's Reading without Nonsense (1997) being a notable exception) I want to suggest that it offers a particularly interesting way to consider children learning at home and one which can be profitably drawn on in rethinking reading.

The acquisition metaphor is one of considerable strength in our society, forming the main understanding of learning deployed in policy, the media, schools and learning institutions as well as common vocabulary. From it flows the familiar school test or public examination which both produces and supports the idea that learning is about the personal gaining of a tangible product. The use of this powerful metaphor is perhaps one of the main reasons as to why, in formal education, assessments have become so extraordinarily important for their supposed power to reveal learning. Tests are vital because they show if learning has or has not taken place, in what measure and to what standard. We are so used to the logic of this way of thinking that it is easy to miss the sleight of thought that has turned the abstract concept of learning into the tangible evidence of the test result. By this means 'learning', an abstract concept, is objectified into a specific entity exemplified by the symbol of the exam certificate. The result is not just learning as an object recognisable through test scores but constitutes a whole orientation towards education as a form of acquisition: we talk about 'the learning process', 'learning outcomes', 'the achievement of literacy' in just such ways. Testing, of course, does not stand alone. Learning is further objectified through expressly designated learning times and spaces, the professionalization of teaching, curriculums, stated learning objectives, and the diagnosis of learning difficulties with their accompanying remedies all of which help to create the idea that learning is something tangible, a thing, which we can see in action, examine, look into and make decisions about

Away from formal education however and away from the usual markers of learning how to distinguish whether learning has happened, if learning is or is not taking place, what does and does not contribute to learning and how long the 'process' of learning takes become questions that have to be re-opened. Indeed, the question of whether it is even helpful to talk about learning in such terms needs to be raised. Although researching home education is not about monitoring learning it also necessarily rests on finding understandings of how learning can be recognised. Learning to read informally presents particular difficulties in terms of identifying what is useful information for research and what is not. Not only is the course of learning something which cannot be directly observed but may also potentially be taking place over the very long term (i.e. a decade or more).

Longitudinal ethnographic study would seem to lend itself to researching children's informal learning, accepting that the people most likely to be able to do this would be parents (for example, Glenda Bissex observed her son Paul learning to read and write over a number of years (Bissex 1980)). But even this is an approach with difficulties. Trying to understand learning means that, in some measure, we must be able to separate out learning from other activities. This is relatively easy to do if we use the school situation but outside formal situations such a separation becomes much harder and this is certainly the case in investigating learning in home education. It is a difficulty illustrated by Alan Thomas' research part of which was based on the prolific diaries kept by a home educating mother over a number of years (Thomas, 1998). Her careful and abundant notes include transcripts of conversations and her own thoughts as well as observations and descriptions of the way her daughter spends her time. The diaries bring home to Thomas the "sheer difficulty of recording instances of learning or experiences which might contribute to learning" (Thomas, 1998, p 80). Diary writing relies on careful observation but also on day to day theorising about how learning takes place. The richness and detail contained in the diaries is obvious from the many excerpts which Thomas quotes, yet the diaries remain as interesting for what is not included as for what is; one example being how the child in question learns to tell the time. This she does with enough dexterity to calculate what the time will be an hour and three quarters hence yet the diary contains only one reference to an incident which involved telling the time. How this little girl learned to tell the time is, it would appear, so wrapped up in other things that the learning left no discernible trail of its own – it was apparently impossible to see her learning as an activity separate to the other things which she did.

As if this were not enough, there is a further difficulty as well. Even in situations where learning can be identified as a separate definable activity there are still important questions about its meaning to answer. The philosophers George Lakoff and Mark Johnson point out in their attempts to differentiate work from non-work that viewing work "as merely a *kind* of activity" leaves out important issues "of who performs it, how he experiences it, and what it means in his life" (Lakoff and Johnson, 1980, p67, italics original). In investigating learning at home we have the same kind of difficulty that a mere activity (such as a child looking at a book) does not answer the questions of who is looking, how are they looking and how does this looking tie into the rest of her or his thinking and life. The asking of these questions and the recognition of their significance is a reminder of some of the words; context, environment, embeddedness, associated with learning as participation. To see learning as something bound into the rest of life brings us closer to this metaphor whilst reminding us of Lakoff and Johnson's point that what we do is only half the story of who we are, how we feel and where we find meaning. These are the thoughts I take forward into the home educators' experiences as the starting point for reconsidering learning to read.

Chapter Three

What is reading?

I now turn to the equally important question of what is reading. As literate adults we read all the time, mostly without considering what it is that we are doing or how it is that we are doing it. Reading is so integral to everyday life that we barely notice it; the literate world is our natural habitat. But any consideration of how children learn to read begs that we ask what reading is and what people are actually doing when they are reading. This is not the straight forward question that it might appear at first glance. On one level it is clear that anyone who can read must know what it is to read, on another level though things are not so easily explained. As Saint Augustine of Hippo said when asked to define grace, "I know until you ask me; when you ask me, I don't know." This chapter begins to explore possible understandings of what reading is by looking at the understandings and practices of home educators.

Understanding reading as a phonetic system

Perhaps the most obvious place to start is with the understanding of reading as a phonetic system; certainly no current discussion of reading education would be complete without an exploration of phonics. It is undoubtedly the most important and influential reading theory of our time. In reading research the most common answer to the question "what is reading?" is that reading is the act of decoding symbols into the spoken words for which they are said to stand. People who are reading are turning symbols that represent sounds back into their original form of speech through a system of phonics.

Mirroring this, when parents were asked about the methods through which they had approached reading with their child, the most commonly occurring theme in their answers was phonics:

> T38: We have a phonetic language. In order to be able to read and comprehend anything at any level, we must learn

the phonetic code rather than memorize a finite number of words!

45Fam: "We've used reading schemes and phonics"

40Fam: "Phonics, The Pirates Reading Scheme".

39Fam: "lots of phonics."

42Fam: "Almost exclusively a series of phonics work books called Explode the Code."

1M: "Looking back it seems clear he worked it out based mainly on phonics".

79M: "He spent hours writing lists of consistently phonetic words."

77M: "Phonics games played on the computer".

Other parents mentioned phonetic techniques such as sounding out words or decoding:

FT9: Using the letter sounds instead of the alphabet letter names

T16M: We began by sounding out letters of the alphabet

T36: We played games and made sounds and put them together and had fun.

A philosophical word on phonics

The phonetic approach to reading embodies the view that writing is speech in symbolic form. The argument forms not only a philosophical basis for understanding reading but also has significant educational bearing. This because the 'speech in symbolic form' argument appears to lead quite naturally to the 'turning letters into sounds' thesis that is such an important mainstream educational principle of learning to read. From it flows further educational consequences such as testing children's reading abilities by asking them to read aloud. So an educational theory has become integrated into a definition of reading and in so doing the question "what is reading?" has been almost totally subsumed into its educative aspects. Sociologically, reading is an educational matter; almost all reading research (including this research) approaches reading through an educational interest and education is the lens through which our mainstream understanding of reading is built. In consequence, as the reading researcher Frank Smith found, "it is impossible to write a book about reading, however detached the intention, without being caught in the crossfire of how reading should be taught" (Smith, 2004, p xi).

The educational interest in phonics defines what reading is, thereby forming a tautological circle in which phonics is the method by which reading has to be taught and learned. The idea that writing is speech in symbolic form has thereby come to form a largely unquestioned base on which to build further educational theory.

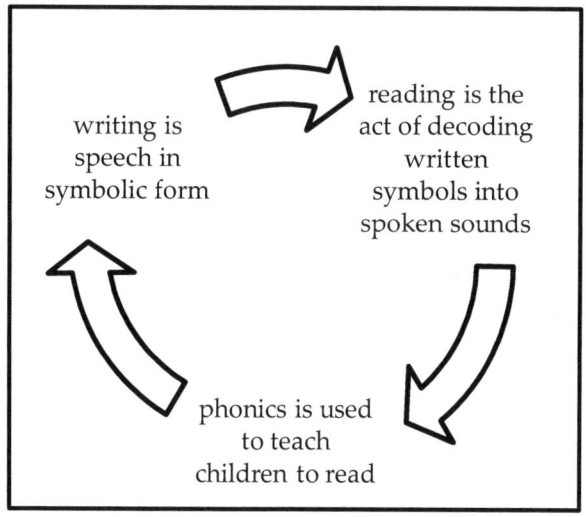

Fig 1

Questioning phonics

Many families took an approach which suggests that although they were happy to go along with the ideas advocated by a phonics approach they were also prepared to be flexible about the extent to which this constituted a definition of reading.

These families used phonic techniques or explanations in an *ad hoc* fashion - in conjunction with other ideas, only at their child's request, in response to appropriate questions, only for a limited period of time or limited in some other kind of a way. In these responses it seems that phonics represents less a system for understanding what reading is and more an occasional perspective and/or sometimes helpful tool.

> 3M: "He did use some simple phonetic books but these were always alongside a vast range of other books".
>
> 7M: "We did talk about sounds that letters make sometimes and sound out words but that was never the focus."
>
> 57F: "verbally teaching some phonics in a very relaxed manner."
>
> 8F: "We have some phonics books…"
>
> 37M: "He also watches PBS Kids television shows that focus on reading skills through word recognition and phonics."

Others brought in phonics in response to children's questions and actions:

> 44Fam: "We answered their questions ("what sound does that make?" "How do you make an 'E' again?" "How do you spell, 'I love you'?"). And we occasionally directed their attention to something ("Oh, look, there's an example of o-u-g-h pronounced the other way")."
>
> 44Fam: "We did convey the rules of phonics and how they could use a combination of phonics and context to work out new words. The majority of this conveyance was in response to their questions or by way of a follow-up comment."
>
> 23M: "We were there to answer any questions he had about reading a word, or phonics or spelling."
>
> 58F: "Just answering questions about letters and their sound."

The restricted contribution of phonics to learning was also communicated through the limited time and application that was spent on the idea:

> 22M: "We used a phonics video programme for two days."
>
> 35M: "He watched some 'educational' TV that used phonics".
>
> 29Fam: "A little bit of phonics".
>
> 31Fam: "He just needed other members of the family to answer a few questions on phonics and then he was able to progress quickly."
>
> 25F: "one short attempt at Hooked on Phonics."
>
> 55F: "We did practice some basic phonics, but she tired of that quickly."
>
> 16F: "talking about letter sounds occasionally, the odd phonics video game. Very little of these things though."

Having been introduced to phonics, the extent to which children actually made use of its ideas was sometimes open to question:

> 52F: "Our daughter listened many times a tale from the French syllabic method "La Planetes des Alphas" but did not follow the method to learn reading."
>
> 2Fam: "Had a little phonics instruction from me but took off on his own from there."
>
> 80M: "Phonics type reading lessons ... provided 'reading lessons' from time to time – a couple of months of lessons and then a couple of months off with no lessons at all between the ages of 6 – 8. His reading took off during an 'off' time (went from beginner reading to reading novels.)"
>
> 34Fam: "He watched the jolly phonics videos, although I suspect he doesn't use that method (it was all news to me watching those, about word sounds)."
>
> 56M: "Teaching some letters and some phonics used an old French reading manual when he was 6 without real

success: He really started to read when he was 9 ½."

Disagreeing with phonics

Where phonics is seen as only a limited element in learning to read or only one out of many possible methods of learning to read, it is not just pedagogy that is being questioned. Definitions of reading are tightly interwoven with educational aspects of reading and to question how reading is taught is also to question the fundamental nature of reading.

The following comments express a definite anti-phonics stance, opposing its connection with reading in theoretical terms:

> 43M: "forget the phonics rubbish (no offence) it is patronising and overly complicated, a letter a week is rubbish and disconnected."
>
> 28M: "The phonics method can confuse some children and does not help children to become good spellers."
>
> 11M: "We never told him to "just sound it out"".
>
> 22Fam: "Nothing about constructing letters, learning phonics, starting 'small' makes sense. It's nonsensical".

One parent expressed her alternative view on phonics by suggesting that decoding is not really reading:

> 15Fam: "Eldest child did not really read until age 12 (was able to do some decoding before that, but not real reading) … youngest is beginning to decode, not reading yet."

Certainly the links between written and spoken language have been strenuously questioned by critics of phonics; there are so many cases in which the 'rules' do not work. A consideration of the English language throws up immediate phonetic anomalies: words that are written differently are pronounced the same (pear and pair), words that are pronounced differently are written the same (read and read), sometimes letters are blended together and sometimes they are not (father and fathead), the pronunciation of some words depends on context (wind and minute) and some letter combinations have a long list of possible pronunciations

(Frank Smith lists eleven different possibilities for the 'ho' combination (Smith 1997)). Many of these anomalies can be traced back through the complicated history of written English to its initial roots as an unwritten language scribed into the alphabet of another language (Latin) and thereafter heavily subjected to centuries long influence from further European languages (Gramley, 2011). This interesting and complicated history does not necessarily preclude the philosophical argument that writing is speech in symbolic form but for some at least, it does beg the efficacy of using phonics methods for the teaching of reading.

However, it is also possible to take the argument further. The late Roy Harris, a professor of linguistics at the University of Oxford, is one of those to put forward an alternative view. Harris, using the difficulties of phonics as a plank in his argument, proposed that "speech and writing are both completely independent, having quite different semiological foundations" (Harris, 2009, p.46). In other words, he saw no clear, given or constant relationship between speech and the written word. Instead he maintained that speech and writing are two separate systems of communication which can be brought together (it is possible to be reading and speaking at the same time) but do not have to be. That speech and writing can be connected on a temporary and active basis does not make them fundamentally linked to one another. Written words can be expressed as speech, either aloud or spoken silently in the mind, but we do not need to do this to be reading. There is no need to utter the words in order to derive meaning from them. His thesis opens up a whole new host of possibilities in considering the reading of home educated children and I will return to his ideas later.

In considering parents' points of view however, the majority of parents connected their disagreement with phonics not with theory but with their own children's experiences:

> 2M: "I also don't feel the need for phonics – I feel my son is confident enough to look at a word and make an intelligent guess about what it means. If he had been taught phonics, I feel this may interfere with his skills

and logic may slow him down."

36Fam: "We read the same stories over and over but I also attempted to force her to learn how to put the letters together to form words instead of just reading and answering her questions because I did not know better "

74M: "He really struggled with the idea of phonetics."

71M: "He spectacularly failed to pick up phonics and early reading skills at school ... made no progress at all through synthetic phonics."

29F: "I tried using phonics but she wasn't interested and couldn't grasp it.

That phonics might interfere with children's own thought process, bore them or simply not suit them was a key theme in such comments:

40M: "He seldom will try to 'sound out' words that he does not know."

68M: "We have some phonics books but he has shown little interest so I don't push it.... I certainly can't force my son to do phonics workbooks etc."

56F: "Jolly Phonics finger books that had been recommended to me. She played with them but didn't seem to get anything out of them ... I realised while trying to help that she really couldn't pick out the sounds in the individual letters. I was surprised by this as advanced speech has been a defining characteristic of my daughter since she was tiny and I found it hard to understand how she could pick up new words so easily yet have so much trouble picking out the sounds within them. It has become apparent that she is a very visual learner for whom phonics makes little sense."

Phonics and the individual

Across the data parents were highly pragmatic about the role of phonics. Parents used phonics if and when it seemed to suit their child as an individual; if their child expressed an interest in phonics or seemed to enjoy phonics.

> 2F: "She liked Jolly Phonics and tracing letters in different media."
>
> 46M: "He naturally picked up on the phonetic side of language."

For other children, phonics simply did not appeal:

> 32M: "My husband tried to do some phonics work with son as he was worried that he wasn't reading at the 'usual' age but didn't persevere with this as son not interested so stopped... I don't think that the phonics trial helped my son as he wasn't ready or interested in reading at that point."
>
> 30F: "Tried phonics and flashcards but she was very resistant."
>
> 40F: "She never liked phonics".
>
> 62F: "I tried phonics with her but with her lack of speech it wasn't that much good as she couldn't say most of the sounds – even when she did start talking."
>
> 56F: "Phonics doesn't suit every child – as a very strong visual learner my daughter finds the individual sounds in words meaningless ... she hears words as a single sound."

This flexible attitude towards phonics represents an important shift in thinking about learning to read. Rather than thinking about the nature of reading, parents are thinking about the nature of their children as learners approaching reading. It is a change with important implications for the question, "what is reading?" On a practical level it puts the individual child at the centre of what it means to learn to read and that individuality becomes the focus for understanding learning. On a theoretical level that children may learn to read in different ways means that a universal definition of reading can no longer be predicated on a theory of reading pedagogy.

Other methods

The main competitors to phonics methods of approaching reading are those which advocate that children learn to recognise whole words. Some parents mentioned, or hinted at, a whole word approach:

> 40M: Reading books the child enjoyed to them, and then first letting the child read the words they could to start and later on reading more and bigger words until they could read the whole story themselves.
>
> 71M: "I used whole word recognition through a scheme called audiblox".
>
> 74M: "I would say he is a whole word reader".
>
> 36Fam: "With the elder child, I followed Mr Doman's method for a while, from ages 1.5-2.5."

Away from phonics however, parents did not on the whole express strong feelings about methods. The following parent described her methods as:

> 77F: "Flashcards, encouragement, lots of good books, bingo games, workbooks"

Such an eclectic approach would appear to be based on expediency rather than theory and is demonstrative of the flexible and individual approaches that marked parents' attitudes across the data as a whole.

The limitations of method

Some parents' comments made it clear that they saw inherent difficulties in approaching reading as any kind of method. A major problem for many was, as discussed above, that they did not consider a method to be something that could be appraised separately from the child using the method:

> 52F: "The method is not important; the important [thing] is that the child likes it."

> 82M: "All methods are good for some children but none is good for everyone."
>
> 55F: "Go with what works for that particular child!"
>
> 31Fam: "I finally came to the conclusion that we should leave methods alone ... 'methods' are only useful if the child is interested in the method as a way to learn to read.".
>
> 23Fam: "There is not a "one–size-fits-all" magic formula."

Another parent considered that a single method could not be expected to provide what a child needed over a period of time:

> 56F: "often requiring different resources to be available at different times rather than following a single 'method' throughout."

Such an evaluation would, again, seem to be rooted in the consideration of the individual child and his or her changing circumstances. And once again the variety of activities parents cited spoke of the importance of interest, enjoyment and activity rather than theoretical method:

> 78F: "Reading lots of books, really simple books, flash cards, phonics books, alphabet and simple word-matching jigsaws, computer games ... but mostly lots and lots of reading."

Methods that don't work

Some parents commented that at least some methods of learning to read were actually detrimental to what they hoped to achieve:

> 49F: "I think that many of the methods for teaching kids to read may take the fun out of reading and then kids give up".
>
> 43F: "Every time I used any method that took the intrinsic value away – flashcards, dumbed-down readers, computer programs etc. it was a long time before joy returned with the desire to learn."
>
> 79M: "Intelligent children learn to read often despite the

methods used."

29M: "We tried numerous different reading 'methods'. Every time a new one was recommended as 'the one' that would teach him to read, we'd buy it and it would fail miserably. It didn't matter what the methodology was behind it – none of it worked for him."

These examples bring us back to philosophical questions of what reading is perceived to be. If reading actually is a method and can be defined through that method then when a child does not learn to read it cannot be that the method has failed. 'Reading' cannot suddenly fall apart as a structure of understanding because some people cannot do it. The continued extension of this argument is that the problem of failure must lie with the child. However, if as parents here have suggested, reading is not a method but is to do with a relationship between reader and reading then it is hardly surprising that some methods will not 'work' for some children.

No method

Some families eschewed any kind of method:

32M: "You don't need to follow a structured plan, as they learn anyway."

66M: "I don't do phonics or anything else."

7F: "I'm sure she provides an example of how perfectly ordinary children can pick up reading skills according to their own enthusiasm and their own timetable without the benefit of rigid phonics schemes, textbooks, or set reading materials."

24Fam: "No phonics, no reading schemes, no flashcards and plenty of Dr Seuss".

38Fam: "We did not use a method."

51F: "Formal lessons are absolutely not required: neither is learning the skills in a particular order."

32F: "No phonics, no flash cards, no traditional teaching

methods were used in our home – for reading or anything else."

An interesting question is begged by the idea of 'no method' about what actually constitutes a method at all. As the following parent found, a method is only a method when it stands in contrast to the rest of life:

> 31Fam: "I read a book by Francoise Boulanger who taught her own children how to read, and as I remember, she didn't really have a particular method but just tried to help them become aware of reading and writing in daily life. So we basically just read lots of books or stories that we liked aloud and borrowed books from the library and used daily opportunities for writing."

In this example the search for a method actually led to the abandonment of method. Instead, everyday life came to be seen as a consequential experience in its own terms rather than as a background to which pedagogy is added. Other parents made similar comments:

> 7Fam: "Living a life style of literacy."

> 12Fam: "Living life in a world where words are everywhere."

> 15Fam: "Given time and exposure children will learn to read and will enjoy it."

Children devising their own method

Some children seemed themselves to settle on what might be described as a 'method':

> 6M: "He learned the letter names by himself and then noticed the letter sounds."

> 40F: "My daughter taught herself to read by 'look and learn' methods."

> 45Fam: "He learned by word recognition."

Such methods are readily recognisable to adults as they fit in with current reading theories however, children's own engagement may well consist of less easily recognised or less approved strategies such as memorising or guessing. Memorising in fact formed an oft cited child led strategy although it holds a contentious place in reading theory.

Memorising

Is recognising or memorising words 'reading'? For ardent phonics advocates it is clearly not. Stainthorp and Hughes (1999) go to the length of inventing non words for reading tests (as do current school reading tests (Department of Education, 2016)) to ensure that the capacity to recognise words does not muddy the waters of ability to decode phonetically. Where the emphasis is placed on technical and cognitive aspects of reading, such as in Stainthorp and Hughes' study, 'real reading' must involve letter sound connections. Memorising words does not depend on this and therefore recognising a word is not a sign of an ability to read. Two problems appear from this argument. Firstly, the definition of reading creates a discrepancy between the way in which beginner readers are expected to read and the way that expert readers read. "Building up a fast and accurate sight vocabulary" (Stainthorp and Hughes, 1999, p14) is acknowledged as necessary for achieving reading fluency yet paradoxically, it is not to be encouraged in beginners. Secondly, in subscribing to the view that 'real reading' must be carried out through a demonstrable and approved thought process a consideration of the child's eye view of reading is effectively denied. A child telling himself a story as he turns the pages of a book may well consider that he is reading and if reading is to be re-thought then understanding children's own views of what they are doing can only enrich that thinking.

Stainthorp and Hughes' view of memory appears to refer to the memorisation of single words. Some parents also commented on the memorisation of separate words as a learning strategy:

> 45Fam: "if he came across a word he didn't know, we only had to tell him once and he knew it after that."

> 22F: "The second time, [rereading] she actually read quite a lot

of it with only a few words needing prompting every time, some every so often and a handful with no help at all. Those words are now imprinted on her brain."

38F: "She started out being able to read her name and then her sister's name, then simple words like Mummy and Daddy, dog and cat etc. She just was able to recognise them.

9M: "He has a phenomenal memory and started out by recognizing whole words that he had seen while we read to him".

Deploying memory in a rather different way, some children learned entire texts by heart. This kind of memorising is generally based on repetitive readings and is rarely mentioned in formal accounts of learning to read; perhaps because so much of the emphasis there lies on progress. In addition, learning 'by rote' has acquired a poor reputation as Ann Browne argues, "learning large numbers of words by rote can also place considerable strain on young children's memories" (Browne, 2009, p 30) and is usually considered a less interesting, less productive activity than word attack approaches. Parents, however, often spoke about memorisation in different and more positive terms. Children who had stories frequently re-read to them often knew them by heart and began their reading experiences from such familiar starting points:

59F: "Over the course of several years, each book was reread a great many times. Most had been memorised, but she still looked at the text while reciting the words."

2M: "He got to know a few books off by heart which he would 'pretend to read' and through this learnt a number of words."

34M: "he liked to read the Ladybird Read-it-Yourself story books ... (I think it was more from memory than actual reading but it gave him confidence).

The dividing line between remembering and reciting the story and reading the text often seemed to fade into a blurred (and insignificant) one.

For these children there seems little purpose in drawing a distinction between recognising, memorising and reading:

> 33M: "He spends a fair amount of time every day looking at his books and will sometimes recite a story he knows well, using the book."
>
> 32Fam: "Younger kids often want to read the same books over and over and over. I believe this really helps them to read, as they learn the story by heart and begin recognising the words they are saying."
>
> 2F: "She seemed to have a natural talent for memorisation and would quote the next sentence of a story before we could read it."
>
> 40F: "My child has an amazing memory for facts. I think she was very interested in books and stories and found learning/memorising the words easy."
>
> 32M: "We'd always read out loud to him and he knew some books by heart word for word so I wonder if that helped him work out the code of reading but don't really know."

Whether or not to consider memorising as 'real' reading is again linked to our definition of what reading is and particularly perhaps to ideas about judging reading ability. If reading is to be assessed by the ability to say aloud a previously unseen text (the test applied by Stainthorp and Hughes in their study of children learning to read at home) then memorising is deliberately precluded as a valid method. In their definition the skill of applying sound to symbols must be undertaken anew every time it is needed. If on the other hand, reading is an inherently contextual familiarity with particular situations and objects then memory might well be a chief means of its accomplishment. Such familiar situations are described by these parents:

> 22F: "I remember laughing that she recognised the world

>
> 'loading' which she'd learnt by looking at it while waiting for various games to load up!"
>
> 81M: "I would not call him a reader yet. He is reading little things on his World of Warcraft game, road signs, movie credits ... all things around us but no books yet."

In these descriptions reading is not a separated out skill but a facet of understanding within a given situation. Here another possibility arises about seeing reading not as a cognitive competence that is specifically acquired and then generally applied but rather as a kind of contextual interpretation which can then in a secondary way become a more general ability. Thus a child might be able to use 'reading' to play a particular computer game, but not be 'reading' in other less familiar situations.

Silent reading

Silent reading is generally taken to be the more advanced version of reading aloud. In his history of reading, Steven Fischer argues that, prior to the Middle Ages, silent reading was a rare and revered art; St Augustine of Hippo coming across his teacher St Ambrose in the act of silent reading was struck by the mystery as well as the rarity of what he saw:

"When he was reading, he drew his eyes along over the leaves, and his heart searched into the sense, but his voice and tongue were silent."

(Augustine of Hippo quoted by Fischer, 2003, p 90)

Certainly in reading education and research it is a huge convenience to suppose that silent reading is something which competent readers do after they have learned to read aloud. It is obviously much easier for a teacher to assess children's reading competence when they are asked to read aloud, although assessing silent reading is not impossible. Similarly, much of what parents know about their children's reading rests on reading aloud. However, some children may not want to read aloud:

34M: "Although he was behind at school the only help they ever gave him was to get a classroom assistant to try and force him to read aloud every day."

46M: "He's not keen on reading aloud anymore and prefers to read to himself unless he finds an especially difficult or exciting bit"

Other children may prefer to read to themselves; perhaps because it is faster:

74M: "I also observed that he seems to be reading faster mentally than he reads out loud. That makes it difficult for him to read out loud."

11F: "She usually 'sounds out' in her head, not out loud."

When children do not read aloud it can be hard to tell how they are progressing:

28Fam: "H taught himself to read at around 5. It was a little harder for me to tell how he was doing as I rarely asked him to read aloud. He is now a fluent reader."

However, the regular assessment of children that takes place in school was often not emulated at home and there were other ways of parents realising whether and how much their child was reading (see Chapter Seven). Certainly the compulsion to read aloud does not exist in the same way at home and those who mentioned it felt it to be unnecessary:

37F: "not interfering and asking them to practice reading for an adult".

39F: "Don't ask them to read out loud if they don't want to."

Listening to children read aloud has also been a major research method for understanding how children go about learning to read. It is much harder to know exactly how children are going about reading when they are doing so silently. As Margaret Clark argues in her study of children who learn to read without teaching, "where children read orally or try out aloud words which cause difficulty, it is possible to study their possible strategies for arriving at meaning; where however, as with many of these children they read silently is often difficult to discover the particular strategies they utilize" (Clark, 1976, p105).

Where reading is closely tied to phonics and deemed to be the converting of text back into spoken language this can only be judged through reading aloud. However, Stainthorp and Hughes (1999) found that vocabulary enlargement can take place through reading silently, recognised in the way that children may know and understand a word which they cannot correctly pronounce. A couple of parents commented on a similar experience:

> 38F: "She'd drop into conversation words that she could only have learnt through reading – something that was even more apparent by her understandably mispronouncing them".

> 46M: "We are aware that this [silent reading] may be 'misreading' or pronouncing some words incorrectly but that comes to light in general conversations and can be corrected then without spoiling or interrupting the story."

In these cases, it would seem that meaning has been attached directly to a written word, the spoken version of which is the last stage in the transaction. This is a disruption of the order imposed by phonics of:

Speech –text– speech

(in which meaning is possible at either of the speech stages although it does not have to be involved at all as with the non-words used in reading tests).

Instead the order established in examples of silent reading such as those above appears to be:

Text – meaning – speech.

Clearly in this order speech is not necessary for meaningful reading. Away from the theory of phonics, silent reading reveals an activity which may be quite different from the phonetic sounding out of words. Fisher argues that "reading silently to oneself often draws on little or no language mediation" (Fisher, 2003, p 337). The symbol on the page can hold an immediate significance without the need for the stepping stone of speech. A child navigating his way around a computer game for example may recognise the word 'play' simply as the symbol that means 'click here to start' thus moving directly from written sign to meaning. As its own medium there is no need for phonological awareness to precede or even accompany such silent reading.

Without this need and as this mother points out, it is quite possible that children could be reading before they are able to speak:

> 62F: "It is hard to say [at what age she began to read] but about 5 reading out loud – she could have been able to do it before that age as she did not speak."

Silent reading is the ultimate realisation of Roy Harris' argument that speech and writing are two separate rather than intertwined systems. It can also shed a potentially new light on the nature of functional literacy in which children are competent users of the written word without adhering to the conventional schooled definitions of what it means to read.

Not knowing

I have argued that how we expect children to learn to read is strongly linked to our understanding of what reading is. But for some parents constructing an argument along these lines is not possible. These are the parents who openly said that they did not know how their children had learned to read:

> 7Fam: "A huge mystery to me."

> 21Fam: "I still don't know [how they learned to read]."

> 51M: "I must be honest and say I don't know HOW he learned to read."

> 2Fam: "Not sure how he learnt to read – seemed to happen overnight!"

> 1Fam: "No clue ... I really have very little idea about how it happens even though I was trained as a Primary School teacher."

These parents constitute an important group in our thinking about reading. Clearly they have not yet heard an explanation of learning to read that fits with their experiences and this rejection of current theory is a means of keeping the question open. It is also a demonstration of a kind of freedom that is perhaps unique to informal education. If education is the process of bringing about some kind of guided change in people then the professional world of education is based on the claims of superior knowledge as to how this is done (Popkewitz, 1987). It is the role of the professional to know how children learn to read and it would be a terrible admission for formal education to announce any kind of ignorance on this point. At home, however, it is not necessary for a parent to hold an understanding of what reading is or how reading happens in the same way. At home the freedom exists to not know or at least to be uncertain and this is the state of mind needed to re-think what reading might be.

This chapter has opened up, through parents own thoughts and words, the question of what reading is and some of the implications of different answers to this question. As can be seen from the spread of data above, there is no emerging consensus on this matter. Home educators hold a variety of opinions on reading. What matters in our further thinking is not who is right and who is wrong in the debate. Rather we simply need to acknowledge that there is more than one way of seeing and more than one way of approaching the meaning of the written word but however we choose to do so, there will be important consequences for how we expect children to learn to read.

Defining what reading is, whether explicitly or implicitly, is a very important first step in developing theories about how it is learned. But there may be other factors at play as well and it is important that we do not forget context. One of the reasons why, as a society, we may have become so wedded to the view that writing is speech in symbolic form may simply be that this leads towards a universal method by which reading can then be taught. In formal education the definition of reading is strongly linked to, if not totally subsumed by, the system through which it is taught. Away from formal schooling and across the spread of questionnaires parents were much more flexible in their thinking about what reading is as expressed through their thoughts and beliefs about how it may be learned. Home educators however are also not people without context. The next chapter explores some of this context by examining, again through the data, some of the theoretical and practical framework surrounding questions of learning relationships at home and whether and how children may be taught to read.

Chapter Four

To teach or not to teach? Structure vs autonomy

Home educators in the UK have long debated the apparent continuum of structure versus autonomy in approaches to education at home. At one end of this continuum lies the kind of formal approach described by Alan Thomas as the "public stereo type of home education" (Thomas, 1998, p 43) in which the child plays the role of pupil to the parent's teacher "who organizes a timetable, teaches lessons, explains what is to be learned, asks and answers questions, sets work and marks it, all during 'school' hours" (Thomas, 1998, p 43). At the other end of the continuum lie autonomous, non- prescriptive families who do not attempt to arrange their children's learning at all. This idea informed my own thinking to the point that I believed I would be able to divide the questionnaire returns into two sets: children who had been taught to read and children who had learned without being taught. The data however revealed a more complex and nuanced picture than that envisaged.

Parents' ideas about learning and the part which teaching or the actions of others might play in that learning formed an obviously important element in how families approached learning to read. However, just as parents were inclined to foreground their child as an individual learner above the idea of reading as a set method, so they were also inclined to temper their ideas about teaching and learning to the circumstances and relationships of their home education. A key influence in shaping the practice which emerged, as well as the beliefs surrounding such practice, were children themselves who exerted considerable agency over the course which their learning took. The result was that identifying 'approaches' from the questionnaires was often not straightforward. Parents who said that they had or had not taught had often done very similar things, or appeared to hold very similar beliefs about learning. What came across instead, from both sides of the supposed structure/autonomous divide, was a deep questioning of the fundamental nature of teaching, flexible attitudes on the part of parents who frequently changed and adapted their ideas in the context of dynamic situations and children who very often had their own strong ideas about reading and about how and when they wanted to explore the written word.

Challenging teaching

When directly asked "Did you (or another family member) teach your child to read?" ninety-one parents attested that they had taught their child to read and one hundred and thirty-three said that they had not. The remaining eighty-seven contributors took issue with the question itself. These challenges took a number of different forms.

Twenty-three contributors gave a qualified response to the question which expressed uncertainty about the use of the term. For example, six respondents replied "not really". Other replies included:

> 68M, 11M: "not explicitly"
>
> 16F "not directly"
>
> 12F "not particularly"
>
> 22M "I wouldn't really say we did"
>
> 59F: "I think I did."

In each case parents seem to be questioning whether or not what could be termed 'teaching' had actually taken place.

Seven more contributors indicated their feelings of inappropriateness about the term by placing it in inverted commas. For example:

> 4F: "We did not 'teach' her to read"
>
> 62M: "Really, he picked it up without any actual 'teaching'".
>
> 22M: "People learn things when they are ready, whether somebody is there to 'teach' them or not"

Other contributors replaced the word 'teach' with a different term such as 'helped' or 'facilitated', 'encouraged', or 'guided'. Substitute terms like 'facilitate' and 'support' suggest a gentler, more child-led approach to adult input than the traditional view of instructive teaching. Such alternative vocabulary, is also found in mainstream literature on literacy learning (e.g. Wells, 1986) and it could be argued that such words simply go more explicitly into what a teacher does; the job of a thoughtful teacher being to support, facilitate, encourage and so on.

However, combined with the other forms of discomfort that clearly surrounded the word there seems to be something larger at stake here. In these ambivalent answers it seemed that parents were both acknowledging their role in their children's learning whilst at the same time questioning the appropriateness of the word 'teach' to describe the part which they felt they had played. Elsewhere, Alan Thomas and I have argued the need for a new vocabulary to describe home education; one explicitly different to the discourse of school education (Thomas and Pattison, 2013). Perhaps the challenge made by parents to the term 'teaching' here can be seen as a further sign that part of the problem in communicating and exploring home education is that we are still continuing to do so through the language of schooling. On the other hand, issues are being raised here which go far beyond the semantic as parents address questions about how learning happens at home and the role of parents and others in that learning.

What's different about teaching at home?

One possible explanation for the unwillingness to use the word 'teach' may be that the term brings with it a history and connotations that actually serve to underline the differences between learning at home and learning in school. 'Teaching' may bring too readily to mind images of chalk and talk; an instructing, assessing arranger of a one way, carefully organized flow of information. Parents may be contrasting home education with their own poor school experiences or the unsatisfactory experiences of children who have been withdrawn from school and in the light of these experiences they may not wish to align their own practices with the control and compulsion associated with institutionalised teaching.

This image of the didactic formal teaching relationship enacted through a set structure and guided by learning objectives was challenged across the data not just by families who said they did not teach but also by families who said they did. Perhaps the differences between learning relationships at home and teaching in school can be summed up as being chiefly about individuality and flexibility.

Individuality

Whatever approach was taken, parents over and over again stressed the importance of recognising their children's individuality:

34Fam: "Be aware of individual differences."

43Fam: "Reading happens differently for different people."

1Fam: "It is very different for different children."

22M: "I think it is different with every person of course."

44M: "It's different for everyone just as learning to walk, or talk is different for everyone."

80M: "Each child is very different in how they learn to read and when they are ready."

74M: "I also think it is important to acknowledge the difference in children."

The foregrounding of individuality in parents' thinking was reflected in the high degree of flexibility across approaches to reading. As noted in the last chapter, thoughts about how children learn to read were more strongly related to the individual nature of the child in question and the social and emotional context of the home rather than to pre-determined, and inevitably static, views on either the nature of reading or of pedagogy.

Flexibility

Across the questionnaires there was a considerable variation in approach but across this variation parents also frequently demonstrated a great deal of flexibility in their thinking about reading. Parents were prepared to change approaches both over time with the same child or between individual children in the same family:

> 45Fam: "We've used a variety of different things, depending on what she wanted to do."
>
> 43Fam: "I have one child who learnt very phonetically by spelling words out and breaking them down into their sounds, and one who learnt by recognising whole words."
>
> 26M: "X hates phonics, but Y quite likes it."
>
> 37M: "We used a variety of methods to find the one that suited best."
>
> 4Fam: "I began with the whole language method after being convinced by Reading Magic by Mem Fox. This wasn't working for eldest so I then switched to Hooked on Phonics."
>
> 9Fam: "I have 12 children all home educated by me; they are all very different. There is no way one size could fit all."

Parents re-considered their strategies, altered their timetables and forecasts and tailored what they did to meet the needs of the moment:

> 5M: "There are many and varied approaches to reading and if one thing doesn't work, try another."
>
> 13M: "No one system works for all, you have to incorporate all methods".
>
> 2F: "When my son appeared less keen on flash cards, I stopped completely for a while, just sharing books with him sitting on my lap."

18M: "I got some early readers and when we used them he quickly said 'reading is boring'. I stopped immediately."

55F: "they will learn to read in the way that best fits them…When the mood is on, go with what works for that particular child!"

13F: "I'd really believed she'd be reading Shakespeare at 2". (child read aged 10)"

81M: "We did flash cards for the alphabet, he completed headsprout.com online when he was 5. That's it and it didn't really teach him to read, but maybe a start for sounding things out. He didn't show any interest in reading for two years after that."

Parents were also prepared to create, or co-create with their children, approaches to reading which suited them:

7F: "Phonics, but my own methods, not from any book or curriculum."

36Fam: "We read the same stories over and over, talked about letters and colored them and drew them and answered questions about words and showed how sounds went together without requesting them to read."

58F: "We have found a Waldorf approach very useful, in combination with Jolly Phonics. In this we introduce phonemes by the Jolly Phonics method, but preface each with Waldorf creative play – giving sounds characters or parts in a story, making pictures involving them etc."

59M: "As I read books I sometimes stop and he tells me the next word. It is recognition of pattern more than anything."

41M: "I also labelled things in the house with their names."

65M: "It progressed over a couple of years mainly in the car. He would ask what various road signs said. He also asked me to sound out number plates on cars."

> 9F: "She was writing random rows of letters and asked me to help her look for words in it (in any language we know)." (Dutch family living in Switzerland and speaking English too.)"
>
> 54F: "She likes to play what we call the 'letter game' with a box of wooden magnetic letters: she says a word she wants to see, we sound out the letters and she picks them out."

Pre-set instruction material may be incorporated within this customised approach but only as it suits child/parent partnerships. Such approaches challenge the instructive nature of traditional teaching and learning models as parents and children pool opinions and interests in the written word and come up with shared ideas about how to explore literacy.

Breaking up the teacher/learner relationship

This high degree of flexibility demonstrates not just the practice but the thinking of home educating parents. Many parents clearly saw themselves as learners in the situation they were in, ready to change their minds, ready to pick up on new ideas, thinking about and questioning the course of learning and reflecting on their experiences:

> 10M: "We have realized he learnt by whole word memory rather than any phonic, sound blend."
>
> 31F: "Just lately I am thinking learning to read involves memorizing words, as some words in the English language aren't spelt the way they sound."
>
> 49M: "A structured system worked for us, with dedication but if I had known what I know since home educating and reading lists, I might have allowed it to just 'happen'. I think it would have done, in time, given the kind of child he is, but a small part of me wonders – IS he the kind of child he is (curious, bright, interested in everything and anything) BECAUSE he learnt to read quickly and early and so a world was opened up to

him."

37Fam: "[methods?] a bit of all with my eldest – less and less with subsequent children (I have 5 children)."

31Fam: "I tried to use the same method as the first son was taught in school, figuring that what had worked for one would work for the other, but that turned out not to be true."

57F: "I learned from my oldest that it's not the end of the world if a child doesn't read by age seven."

Even in families with many children, parents were not using their experience to build methods or theories on reading but were, on the contrary, in a continual reactive and open state of mind themselves. The idea of the all-knowing teacher, omniscient in a given subject and guiding the reliant child carefully forward on a tried and tested pathway is replaced by individuals participating in an experimentally natured, joint collaboration. As this parent put it:

26M: "I wouldn't characterise the process as either us (his parents) teaching him or him teaching himself to read. We see it more as a co-operative venture"

Continuing to break away from the idea of a single teacher acting as a conduit for knowledge, some parents pointed out the collective nature of learning to read at home in which numerous family members, including siblings, could be involved:

10F: "We all participated in part",

64M: "The whole family helped him (mum, dad, sister and two brothers), but he mostly taught himself"

45Fam: "The whole family facilitated her to teach herself",

23Fam: "We all help each other".

67M: "Myself and my husband …"

38Fam: "I taught/assisted them and they taught/assisted each other."

8F: "Me, my husband and my mother have all 'assisted' her."

Help or information received from a number of sources can be rather different to information received from a single source. Alan Thomas and I have previously discussed the difference between the pre-digested and carefully sequenced information provided by planned teaching as opposed to the piecemeal and ad hoc information that is scattered through everyday life (Thomas and Pattison, 2007). Information from a variety of sources is likely to contain at least some elements of the latter requiring to be sorted and assessed, perhaps contradictions addressed or gaps filled as children go about constructing and refining their own knowledge and feeding new information and experiences into their emergent thinking.

Reading as cultural participation

The kinds of situations described above are not ones of didactic teaching. Instead they might be more accurately expressed through ideas of social or community based learning in which no one teacher takes responsibility for a child's learning but instead a kind of cultural fostering takes place. This type of learning is described in a highly influential book entitled "Situated Learning: Legitimate Peripheral Participation" written by social anthropologist Jean Lave and computer scientist Etienne Wenger (Lave & Wenger, 1991). The authors describe a number of different types of apprenticeships in which beginners in skills such as tailoring gradually become experts in their chosen fields. Apprentices are acknowledged from the outset as part of a 'community of practice' of professionals although they are not yet full participants. Instead their participation is peripheral; initially they merely observe, then they begin to perform simple fringe tasks, working gradually up through increasing skill levels until they too are masters. The relationship between expert and newcomer is aimed at fostering this participation rather than being based on the directive pedagogy of formal schooling. Although learning clearly takes place, Lave and Wenger emphasise that this is through increasing participation in practices which they see as social rather than as examples of abstract learning acquired through cognitive processes. According to them it is the relationships which pertain between expert and beginner; the sharing of resources, experiences and problem solving techniques which underpin learning. Participation in the group rather than individually held theoretical knowledge marks the transition to expert.

The ideas of legitimate peripheral participation and communities of practice can be transferred to a family context in which children are fully accepted from (or before) birth as group members and become gradually incorporated into the cultural practices of family life first as observers, then as minimal and finally fully fledged participants. (The nature of the transference from passive to active, peripheral to full functioning in terms of learning to read is one deserving of further interrogation (Pattison forthcoming)). Alan Thomas and I have also discussed these ideas elsewhere both in terms of participation in simple cultural patterns such as housework and social practices (Thomas and Pattison, 2007) and in terms of acquiring particular values and norms via the hidden curriculum in schools (Pattison and Thomas, 2016). In a similar vein but with specific regard to literacy Frank Smith has described how children "join the literacy club" (Smith, 1997, p 113). He suggests that in a situation, such as a family, it is accepted that new comers (children) will become fully active members of the club who will behave like other members of the club and who will value what those members value. There is an overwhelming expectation that children will read and because of this expectation, children see themselves as readers and are motivated to join in (with assistance where required) the activities of the 'club'. In these theories there is much emphasis on meeting innate curiosity and exploration with adult led practices to foster and encourage them. Such practices as looking at books, turning pages, being read to, taking a book out of the library are widely recognized as being part of the process of emergent literacy and are seen as contributing to reading prowess in main stream thinking (Weinberger, 1996) although they are always backed with direct teaching as well (Stainthorp and Hughes, 1999).

Taken to its logical conclusion, viewing families as communities of literacy practice recasts reading, not as a cognitive skill to be addressed through the metaphors of personal acquisition, but as a social practice that is carried out and is meaningful within a particular social and cultural setting. Considering families as communities of practice is a way of contextualizing learning at home so that children can be seen as becoming participants in the literate world that already exists around them. The following quotes describe the environment of literacy and some of the possible influences of families as communities of practice:

> 5F: "Reading is important to the adults in our house…"
>
> 2F: "We are a musical family and did a lot of singing. She learned solfa very young and actually learned to read music before the alphabet."
>
> 26F: "She watches us read"
>
> 59M: "He also watches other kids read and learns from them."
>
> 74M: "My home is full of books all around the home. Just exposing your children to see you read, makes them want to join and engage in lively debates."
>
> 48M: "It is critically important that the child see others around them greatly enjoying reading – it seems to set an expectation that they will eventually too."
>
> 32F: "Subsequent children learned much from siblings."

As with Lave and Wenger's professionals, parents have their own literate lives to pursue and their own reasons for using literacy. The part they play is not to teach children knowledge and reading skills but to allow their peripheral participation in the literate life which is already going on around them. Parents who saw their actions as contributing to their child's learning but not constituting teaching can be understood within the framework of the community of practice.

One parent explicitly described this as an apprenticeship relationship:

5Fam: "Apprenticeship with books of all types."

Others, by eschewing the term 'teach' in favour of describing literacy activities like reading to children, suggested more implicitly that this is what might be happening:

54M: "He basically learnt as we read to him."

13M: "My husband and I read to him."

43M: "We just read books to him."

7M: "We simply read a lot of books together"

34F: "She was read to so frequently, it's hard to say."

2F: "We read to her, she then started reading to us."

The community of literacy practice can clearly be seen as being much wider than the home and as encompassing much more than such focussed activities as reading aloud to children. Parents also made reference to the broader culture of literacy which prevails in modern society and to the cultural, social and emotional imperatives that exist to join it:

14M: "The printed word is so embedded in our society and culture he sees it and reads it whenever and wherever it interests him."

20F: "In the presence of a rich language environment where the printed word is present and used, children come to reading on their own."

27F: "I always remember my daughter picking up very quickly on the big bright lights of the supermarket names!"

12M: "Menus – looking for those items that have French fries as sides, books – those that have interesting captions that mom passes over."

14M: "The desire to learn anything culturally or socially based is inherently human."

Of course in main stream education a literate environment and literate practices such as reading aloud to children are seen as very important. Modelling and involving children in literacy is strongly encouraged as an educational device to back up formal teaching in school. However, it is important to note that taking a community of practice perspective confers a completely different intention and theoretical context on what may appear at first glance to be the 'same' situation or the 'same' activity. This is an important point which will be revisited in the next chapter.

Challenging the concept of teaching

So far this chapter has considered how the word 'teaching' may bring to mind images which do not necessarily reflect well the kind of relationships and interaction in home educating families. On these grounds it is possible to question and even reject the idea of teaching at home. Parents may want to differentiate between the practices that go with managing a class of 30 children within the framework of a set timetable and curriculum and those which go with teaching one, two, three or other small numbers of children within the relaxed intellectual and temporal context of home. However, the rejection of the idea of teaching may go beyond renouncing the practices and styles that characterise typical formal teaching. It may also signify a denunciation of the conceptual understandings on which the very idea of teaching is based.

Teaching and learning relationships in schools and other educational establishments are generally clear cut and well characterised. Teachers do certain things and behave in certain ways whilst pupils and students do other things and behave in different ways. Roles are distinct both in terms of teacher and student's different relationships to each other and to their subject matter. Behind these roles lies the thinking and reasoning that constitute our educational theories. Teacher and pupil roles are a practical expression of how learning is considered to happen and how learning is considered to happen reveals a more fundamental understanding of how the human mind is believed to work. As a result of these links we cannot separate out teaching from our understanding of a much bigger picture. Teaching cannot be adequately seen as simply a bundle of professional practices or strategies of behaving. Instead we need to acknowledge that any definition of teaching is also a comment on how we understand both people and knowledge. Indeed, the question is much bigger than education – it is about what it means to be a person.

Philosophers of education may be much engaged with this kind of thinking but on the whole education systems are not. Instead practices of teaching are based on largely unquestioned assumptions about how minds operate with the overt attention concentrated on how teaching can best mediate the relationships between knowledge on the one hand and people on the other as if these things are already givens (Blake et al, 2000). Teaching, learning and knowledge are presented as a bundle of interrelated and inter-defined elements so that each element is also a comment on the other two. When we talk about learning as a process of acquisition then it makes sense to talk about teaching as a process of delivering or transmitting and knowledge as a discrete heap of information that can be transferred from one person to another; if we think about learners building knowledge then it dovetails to talk about teachers co-constructing that knowledge and knowledge being something that can be incrementally gathered and so on.

Once these interrelationships are established teaching becomes the practical matter of enacting them so, for example, how knowledge can best be delivered becomes a question of what actions should be taken or which words should be said. At this point, teaching has passed from being a theoretical idea about the nature of the human mind to being a material reality; something that we can do and see others do. Teaching has become an activity in its own right with identifiable features which in turn can be observed, studied, tested, measured, written about. More than this teaching can itself be taught so that we can create teachers - our abstract theorising about how the human brain works has now resulted in more than just some practices of behaving, it is now personified, a professional identity - a person who is a teacher. A theoretical understanding of how people might think has been transmuted into the empirical reality of a teacher standing in front of a class explaining how a combustion engine works through a power point presentation or sitting in a group playing a phonics game about what sounds various letter blends make. Teaching has become a real lived experience with its own far reaching implications for educational thinking including the "classic assumption ... that children learn because they are taught" (Trevarthen, 1995, p97).

To question teaching is not just to question a set of practices but also to question a whole set of fundamental ideas about learning and knowledge, about the nature of human beings. It is difficult territory to advance into but some of the ideas raised by parents through this data beg that we open our minds to just such a consideration.

If we follow the theory of mind behind teaching then certain actions, labelled teaching, may be seen to lead to certain outcomes understood as learning. However, if we challenge the idea that human minds operate in this way then the cause and effect link between teaching and learning is broken. The following quotes illustrate how situations may be differently interpreted if a different philosophical viewpoint is brought to bear on them:

> 7F: "Sometimes after watching these programmes she'd like us to play games that echoed the songs and pictures she'd just been watching, so (very occasionally to be honest) we'd write and illustrate a word on her magic drawing board, such as "sun" and then extend it to "sunny" or "sunshine". We'd read them out in silly voices which made her giggle. This is as close to a reading scheme as she ever undertook. Therefore, it was unstructured and, fundamentally play. We certainly didn't think we were actively teaching her anything."

40F: "I always read books to my child, and often put my finger under the words as I read. I did this just to help my daughter be interested in books. By age 3 she could read quite a lot of easy children's books. I don't think I taught her, but rather she taught herself."

38F: "We did play a lot of games that involved recognising and matching words not with the intention of her learning anything from them."

What might look like teaching from a particular perspective may be understood quite differently from a different set of ideas about what learning is and how minds operate. The understanding that informs action, rather than the actions themselves, is what makes the teaching/learning relationship possible and 'real'. Instruction is a perceived possibility based on very particular understandings about how human beings think and function. Conversely, if our theory constructs learning differently then the same 'evidence' will point towards quite a different interpretation. This becomes particularly clear when we turn to the role which the home educated children play in their own learning.

Children's agency: resisting, requesting and doing it for yourself

So far this chapter has discussed the ways in which parents' words and actions challenge mainstream ideas about teaching and its place in learning. However, perhaps the strongest influence on parents' thinking and actions is that of children themselves and their reactions to reading. Parents sometimes found that their expectations of teaching were confounded by the actions and responses of children. Sometimes parents who had expected to teach their children found that teaching rejected or pre-empted. Sometimes parents who had not explicitly set out to teach found their child requesting their active engagement in reading. And some parents reflecting back on their teaching initiatives found themselves questioning their experiences and understandings about what had actually happened in and through that process.

Teaching being rejected

In these cases, parents intended to teach and began to do so only to find that children were not interested or that their efforts simply did not inspire their off-spring:

> 41Fam: "I started to 'teach' her at age four but she wasn't interested. Decided to leave her alone…"
>
> 37Fam: "Tried [to teach] but gave up …I felt that what they wanted to spend time doing (playing) was obviously more important."
>
> 29F: "I tried using phonics but she wasn't interested and couldn't grasp it."

Sometimes the decision to give up seemed to be a mutual one:

> 46Fam: "When she was 5 we briefly tried "how to teach your child to read in 100 easy lessons," which turned out to be torture for both of us."
>
> 29Fam: "A. read later than her big sister so I started to worry and sit down and try to 'do phonics' with her. That failed miserably and turned her off reading. I finally just waited and went back to reading to her."

In other instances, the rejection of teaching was much more forthright:

> 19M: "He resisted any attempts on my part to get him to read."
>
> 17M: "My son was very resistant to 'being taught' when he left kindergarten."
>
> 50M: "I started fairly structured 'teaching' when my son was 5 but it was so resisted by him."
>
> 30F: "Tried phonics and flashcards but was very resistant… she knew her letters, but resisted any form of formal teaching"

13F: "She would become hysterical at any attempts by me [to teach her]."

73M: "The more I tried to 'help' my son learn to read, the more he resisted."

36Fam: "[She] developed a strong antipathy toward anything resembling instruction in reading. ... she would actually get up from my lap and leave if I so much as ran my finger under the words while reading to her. One could not comment on oddities of spelling, or similarities of sounds, or any such thing. If one came upon her looking at a book, she would instantly close it and walk away.

61F: "At age 4 years 3 months she said she didn't want to learn to read."

As Boaz Tsabar (2014) notes, resistance to the authority of education is commonplace and a good deal of educational practice is concerned with how this resistance can best be managed. David Lancy (2014) similarly argues that "the greatest problem facing schools in the USA seems to be persuading students that they should want to be there" (Lancy, 2014, p333). As Tsabar points out a grounding principle of all traditional educational ideologies is that, "unwillingness to learn ... must be subdued as a condition for successful educational action" (Tsabar, 2014, p31). This type of thinking argues that children's negative feelings towards instruction must be tackled and reversed (although Tsabar interestingly argues that resistance should be seen as an emancipatory force, an evaluation which could be seen to fit some of the descriptions above). Some parents did talk about pushing through children's reluctance:

66F: "A few of them [family of 8 children] would fight me in the beginning and tell me it was 'too hard', but then they would persevere (with some coercion on my part), and the light would switch on in their heads when they realized they had discovered how to read!"

36Fam: "We read the same stories over and over but I also

attempted to force her to learn how to put the letters together to form words instead of just reading and answering her questions because I did not know better "

31F: "I try for up to one hour a day for reading and writing. ... I think she sees it as a chore at the moment."

However other parents were not prepared to take on the struggle and by far the most common reaction to children's resistance was for parents to back off and wait for the child to take the lead at some point in the future:

76F: "WAIT, WAIT, WAIT"

65 M: "When we try to pound the how to of reading into boys before they are ready, it makes them very frustrated. If you can wait until they are mature enough, it can happen very quickly, painlessly."

64F: "[I learned] not to force a child to read."

60M: "I think reading is better left to come naturally when a child is ready."

35F: "it [teaching] doesn't do any good if the child isn't interested."

It is important to see in these accounts that it is teaching which is being resisted; not necessarily learning. In school these two ideas (as discussed above) may be too conceptually intertwined to separate but at home rejecting teaching did not necessarily mean that children were not learning.

Requesting

As well as rejecting teaching, children also sometimes asked for it. However, it seems that when children requested help they were not casting themselves in the role of a passive learner wanting a parent to manage the learning situation for them. Instead they asked specifically for what they required in the facilitation of an on-going relationship with literacy. Generally, this took the form of either a parent being requested to read for them or to answer questions:

83M: "He keeps asking me to read with him."

82M: "Reading road signs to him when he asked."

79M: "The first 2 finished the course in 18 months (its supposedly a 3 – 4 year course) with no pressure it became fun and they asked to do it."

37M: "We facilitate when we are asked by him for assistance"

10Fam: "I just answered questions when asked."

11Fam: [They] "asked for help from me when needed."

44Fam: "Mainly we answered their questions"

59F: "I was available to answer her constant questions. The process was child-led but the level of involvement from me was very high."

55F: "She very much wanted me to work with her, so I did! ... I can't say that I really taught her. She wanted my help so I gave it."

33M: "What I think really works is that any instruction that we give is always at his request."

Children could also be quite explicit about when enough teaching was enough:

44M: "He did ask me once if I could teach him but that lasted about a week and he quickly changed his mind."

73M: "We did the book *The One Stop Reader* when he asked me if he could learn to read (at the age of 8). But he stopped me half way through and announced he could read."

In these examples parents do not appear to be acting as teachers who manage or control the learning process. Instead they are human resources for their children's learning to be used as and when desired, whilst it is children who decide what they are interested in and how to further that interest.

Self-teaching

Perhaps the single biggest challenge to the idea of teaching came from the large group of contributors who asserted that their children had taught themselves to read. Some parents saw themselves as enabling this to happen and therefore playing an active part in the process:

> 54F: "I would say she is semi-teaching herself with guidance from my husband and I."
>
> 45F: "We help them teach themselves and give them plenty of chance to practice."

For others, self-teaching went hand in hand with requesting help. In these cases, children appeared to self-manage the process of learning to read at least partly through specifying and recruiting the help they wanted from their parents:

> 11Fm: "It was a group effort (the kids and mine) as they more or less taught themselves and asked for help from me when needed"
>
> 5Fam: "They taught themselves and I facilitated."
>
> 22F: "She taught herself with help (when asked for) from her mother."

For others parental involvement was even more minimal:

> 19F: "I would say she taught herself."
>
> 42Fam: [My husband said to me] "you didn't teach them. They taught themselves. You just knew when to get out of the way."
>
> 18Fam: "My four eldest have taught themselves to read"

Other parents argued that it was specifically their contribution to leave children alone:

> 17F: "It is best when adults are in the background, only offering assistance when asked."
>
> 24F: "I purposely tried to stay out of it."
>
> 29F: "Leave them to it."
>
> 34F: "I believe a child needs to do it on their own."

36F: "Not interfering basically."

37F: "Not interfering"

38F: "Letting her do it in her own time and in her own way."

57M: "It worked better if I didn't interfere."

65M: "Get out of their way."

Such a strategy might be called positive non-interference and stands in contrast to the conventional interventions of education in which children are to be helped, guided and supported almost continuously by adults towards inevitably adult goals.

Pre-empting teaching

Sometimes the course of learning was so unobtrusive that parents did not recognize that it was happening at all and were taken by surprise when they offered instruction which had by then become irrelevant. In the following examples parents who had expected to teach found that children had pre-empted their plans:

6M: "I knew that letters were the first thing taught in kindergarten so I was going to start here until I realized he already knew the letters. Then, I was going to teach the letter sounds and I realised he already knew them. Then, I was going to move on to sight words since he knew letters and sounds already. I never got the chance. One day when he was sitting looking at a joke book, I realized he was reading it."

43M: "When I withdrew him from school I worried that I should teach him to read and how would I afford the 'easy readers' … ha! … In the time I was worrying he had learned to read, in a couple of weeks of being out of school I asked him what a word in a book was, expecting 'the'. He read out 'the countries of Oceania and Australasia are …' I can't remember the rest but I decided then not to worry."

43F: "She was reading at age 5 (which was kind of disappointing as I was sort of hoping to apply the

Steiner methodology - however, I'm not disappointed now)."

28Fam: "I was a little disappointed at first that my kids didn't seem to need me to help them learn to read, but I got over it!"

Other parents began teaching in a fairly conventional sense only to find that their children appeared to be learning independently of that teaching:

30Fam: "began a Christian phonics program at age four, reading it by himself in one month, far more advanced than where we were at in the program."

50F: "tried a Christian phonics program at age four, progressed nicely, yet child reading at a higher level by age five than the program teaching guide."

62F: "I use a curriculum called Sonlight – which I buy in from the USA and it has a sort of phonics system but with small books to start with – with one word on each page etc and build up using the various 'sounds' of the alphabet etc ... just as I was beginning to teach her she suddenly launched into reading by herself – reading words that I had either never read to her or she had never seen before really easily."

76M: "When he showed an interest, we told him about letter sounds and did some simple phonics. He went from having a grasp of simple phonetic words to being able to read above grade level extremely quickly although he hadn't started to read at all before the age of 7."

71M: "I used a scheme called 'toe by toe' but we only did the first 1/3 of it as his reading was taking off so much by then that it became a pointless chore."

In a somewhat similar vein, these parents gave up teaching as its effectiveness appeared to run out, only to find that the problems apparently resolved themselves without teaching:

3Fam: "I actually only taught him the technique up to a point. We hit a brick wall with words that had more than 2 syllables and so I left it, only to discover that he started reading long words by himself a month later."

30Fam: "tried to use a Christian phonics program, flashcards, but she would cry and get depressed so I left it thinking I would try again around age six, but she was reading before that."

Moving from teaching to learning

So far this chapter has discussed the influences which children have themselves had on their own paths to reading. These range from rejecting teaching to co-creating reading practices with their parents to independent self-teaching including managing their parents as resources in that process. These examples serve to shift the theoretical emphasis from teaching to learning; a theme overtly taken up by the following parents:

11M: "He learned to read, we didn't explicitly teach him"

12M: "My child learned to read because it was what he wanted to do. I couldn't stop him if I wanted to."

25Fam: "They learned rather than being taught."

6F: "She LEARNED how to read"

51F: "I helped her learn, I didn't 'teach' her."

56F: "I am trying to help her learn to read"

35Fam: "I guess they learned ..."

The social anthropologist David Lancy looking across a wide sweep of ethnographic evidence puts forward the argument "that active or direct teaching/instruction is rare in cultural transmission" (Lancy, 2014, p 205). He goes on to assert that "one of the most unequivocal findings re childhood from the ethnographic record is children learning their culture without teaching" (Lancy, 2014, p 209 italics original). Indeed, active teaching is a rarity or at least very strategically used away from

Western society, necessitating as it does the concentrated overseeing from an adult who is then unable to pursue his or her own ends (Lancy, 2014). More than this, what would be taken in the West as constituting important, if not crucial steps in learning, may be regarded elsewhere as wasteful of time or resources or simply as children being nuisances in adult spaces. Lancy describes a range of reactions to child imitation and initiation of activities. The Moose of West Africa for example, treat children who are mis-performing a task (which we might perceive as valuable playing or imitating) with calls to stop or threats of punishment. Nevertheless, such children are competent learners and Lancy cites examples of cultural learning such as behaviour patterns and craft skills with observation being a key learning method. He does not however include the kinds of subject matter such as reading which we would designate as cognitive and associate with the school curriculum.

As discussed in previous chapters, the idea that reading needs to be taught is closely tied to its construction as a cognitive skill; the overwhelming understanding of reading as it occurs in the modern, Western world (see for example UNESCO, 2006). This means that learning to read is understood as a dialectical process between subject (the child) and object (the text). The text constitutes a system which exists in its own right, independently of the child but which can be made meaningful when mapped onto a second system which exists for the child as personal knowledge. Thus interdependencies of understanding are created between the external and internal systems; the locus of reading is 'in the head' and occurs within a child's own thinking capacity (Ferreiro 1985). The metaphors of acquisition and ownership are implicitly (and sometimes explicitly) present in such accounts. To be a successful reader the individual child needs to be in possession of the internal system which will make sense of the written text.

In contrast to this view, I have suggested that we explore the idea of reading as a cultural practice, rather than a cognitive skill. Doing so allows for an alignment of the home educating families' experiences with Lancy's assertion that cultural learning results not from an "adult-directed 'transfer of cultural knowledge'" (Lancy, 2014, p 209) but through the development of social practices in context as they are initiated by children themselves. Parents' emphasis on the culture of literacy and the pro-activity of children as learners are an echo of this argument:

> 9Fam: "Reading is a fundamental skill that will be acquired in a world where the written word is all around them."

> 3Fam: "It seems to me that if a child is surrounded by reading material, very little, if any, teaching is necessary."

> 18M: "It is very difficult to not learn to read in our society."

> 28M: "I believe that in this information rich age every child WILL learn to read in their own way and at their own pace, regardless of methods used or actual 'teaching'."

> 35M: "It is part of what seems to be an internal motivation to master the world around them and because our culture uses the written word, it just happens."

> 78M: "If you are surrounded by things to read, you will learn to read."

These thoughts suggest children's predilection to engage with the community of practice of literacy in which they are living; bearing out the words of Olson that "culture is learned less because of the pedagogical efforts of the adults than because of the predispositions, agency and intentionality of the children" (Olson, 2009, p 11).

Such strong expressions of agency on the part of children can be taken to indicate what we might gloss as children's ownership of their own learning. This ownership, in contrast to the ideas of acquisition, is not about children possessing certain cognitive structures but is rather about them being in control of their own behaviours and actions and the feelings which guide these, such as interest, boredom or curiosity. In formal education the idea of children 'owning' their learning is very often couched as being a goal orientated drive in which learners use "such self-regulatory processes as goal setting, self-monitoring, self-evaluation, and strategy use" (Zimmerman, 2000, p87). Some children certainly did seem to set out to learn to read and there were cases where learning appeared to be an overtly self-managed process as this young man described of himself:

> 38M: "It got to the point where there were too many things in daily life that needed reading ... it was not at the top of the list of things to learn until I was 12."

This type of scenario suggests an explicit learning aim and a specific desire, if not strategy, to accomplish that aim. However, much of the time motivation seemed to have a different horizon; flowing from immediate concerns such as the need or desire to engage with different types of written material, to emulate others or to participate in ongoing aspects of social life as opposed to a drive to master a general ability. A deeper exploration of the role of motivation in learning to read is addressed in a later chapter.

Questioning the value of teaching

Of the parents who set out to teach their children, some came to question what they had done and what the effect of their actions had been. Even where teaching is taking place, with co-operation and even enjoyment, it is not necessarily easy to say exactly what can be designated as a consequence of that action:

> 52F: "I don't believe in 'teaching' so much as 'facilitating' someone's learning. You can make someone memorize anything though, but that doesn't mean they understand it and can act successfully and reliably on that memorized information."

> 72M: "It's hard to say if I taught him or if he just absorbed the skills himself from time spent reading together."

> 36Fam: "With the elder child, I followed Mr Doman's method for a while, from ages 1.5-2.5. She quite enjoyed it, but I should state that it was never my impression that she could actually read the flash cards, that is, she did not decipher, just learned to recognize shapes. It was

uncomfortably like teaching a parrot to "talk". However, because she enjoyed it, we continued up until the point where she was supposed to be learning to read sentences. She lost all interest at that point, and turned to an enthusiasm for learning the names and sounds of individual letters. Doman, as one may know, disapproves of this pursuit, but I followed her lead and put aside the flash cards. She spent the year 2.5-3.5 gleefully reading aloud letters wherever she saw them. Then, quite abruptly, or so it seemed to me, she began to read independently. She moved from deciphering very simple board books to being able to read absolutely anything - aloud, with different voices for different characters - in about two months. I have never been able to decide what role the Doman training played in all this."

Some parents felt that their efforts to teach actually resulted in the opposite to the desired effect:

26F: "We tried [to teach] before embracing unschooling. ... She still doesn't read. I feel that the 'encouraging' we did has hurt her desire to learn. She now thinks of it as hard and not fun. Yet she continues to learn more and more without our help."

36Fam: "I tried to teach her to read but ultimately she learned at her own pace and on her own. I feel I interfered with her natural process."

71M: "Although I did attempt to 'teach' him, I really think he has learned despite me and certainly despite the dreaded school schemes simply through having time to explore things he wanted or needed to read."

78M: "I put a huge amount of pressure on my son when he was 5 and 6 to learn to read – he knew the alphabet and could sound out words, but wasn't ready for the next step. I think a lot of that was because I was putting pressure on him so 'learning to read' became a big black cloud for him. It took me backing off, a year or two of no pressure and him to get into chapter book series which he could read but the story was also interesting enough for him."

43F: "Every time I used any method that took the intrinsic value away – flash cards, dumbed-down readers, computer programs etc. it was a long time before joy returned with the desire to learn."

25F: "We made an attempt at learning to read using Hooked on Phonics but it produced a lot of anxiety so we dropped it after 2 or 3 unfruitful attempts at lessons."

56F: "My fumbling around for the best ways to help her may have assisted and encouraged her sometimes, but I can certainly think of times when they undoubtedly hindered too!"

Finally, some parents questioned whether teaching had any legitimate place at all in learning to read:

14F: "I don't think someone else could take credit for teaching someone to read – only perhaps for providing the necessary conditions."

32Fam: "We can teach them all we want, but like so many skills and milestones they will achieve it when they are developmentally ready. We could save a lot of time and turmoil for both parties if we just WAITED for the child to be older before we push reading on them."

Opinions of teaching and its efficacy here are shading into parents' other concerns; particularly the view that being able to read was not, by itself, a worthy enough goal. Behind many of the opinions expressed about learning and teaching lay hopes and ideals not encapsulated by teaching – no matter how effective. The following parent questioned explicitly that teaching could ever achieve what she clearly felt to be the goal of literacy – a spontaneous love of reading:

38Fam: "'Teaching' does not create a love of reading. A desire and natural curiosity that is 'aided and abetted' drives a natural reader."

Others felt that what they were attempting to do could not be described in terms of teaching a skill but rather of something deeper, more emotionally than cognitively based:

50F: "to motivate the love of learning and reading."

26F: "fostering a love of learning anything, including reading."

2M: "I feel that there is no need to teach it, only to perhaps encourage a love of reading."

5M: "turn[ing] them into people who love to read … "

Talk of the love of reading turns the metaphor onto new ground. Reading is no longer something that is acquired, or even participated in; it is not an independently existing skill or piece of knowledge. Instead it is an object of emotional attachment which can become something that someone is, an identity; 'a reader', 'a lover' of literature. The emphasis here has turned from what children know to what kind of person they are and how it is that they have become that person.

The challenges to 'teaching', both the word itself and the theory behind it, permeate the questionnaire responses and push deeply and widely into a core concept of education. Challenges to what is meant by teaching arose across the questionnaire responses; directly to be sure but also in practical ways as children and their families found novel and individual ways to explore reading and literacy. In doing so many moved away from didactic teaching relationships to more diffuse patterns of engagement and to immediate, rather than mediated relationships with the written word themselves. This in turn questions transmission models of learning based on the transference of fixed subject matter. Instead the idea of the learner, shaping and defining both his or her own subject matter and means of engagement begins to rise to the fore and with it the idea of reading as an emotional engagement and being a reader as an identity.

Chapter Five

What do families do?

The previous chapter discussed how many families challenged conventional ideas about teaching and being taught. Parents were inventive and flexible in their approaches to reading and children were pro-active and creative in their explorations, both independently and in partnership with their parents. All this makes for a dynamic mix in which the standard understanding of learning being a response to teaching often seems to disappear from view. Nevertheless, whether they felt that they had taught or not, most parents did feel that they had been or were importantly involved in their children's literacy lives. Most parents had strong ideas about which activities or aspects of the environment had been influential in their children's learning even if they were still unable to say how learning had occurred.

Reading aloud

When parents were asked what they felt had contributed to their child learning to read the most often cited factor was reading aloud. The vast majority of parents said that they did or had read aloud to their child. They are certainly not alone in considering reading aloud to be important, if not critical, in children's reading lives. Advice to read to children is widespread and common and reading aloud to children has become part of the common cultural sense of learning to read. A BBC website for instance tells parents "Reading with your child is vital. Research shows that it's the single most important thing you can do to help your child's education" (BBC, 2012). Yet whilst most parents were convinced that reading aloud to children is important, they were not always agreed on why this should be so.

Reading aloud as a form of transmission

Some parents talked about reading aloud as a means of transmitting and acquiring the connections between written and spoken words. Pointing out words or running a finger under the text whilst reading were most often cited as ways of creating and highlighting the connections between speaking and reading:

> 24Fam: "We read some words together, I pointed at the words. She made the connections between the sounds I made and the shapes on the page."
>
> 14Fam: "I think it was important that we read to them a lot, and ran our finger along the line as we read."
>
> 7F: "We'd always read to [our daughter] and I usually ensured I tracked the words with my fingertip as I read them aloud."
>
> 19F: "When reading to her I would always move my finger along the text as I read."

For others, reading aloud seemed to offer opportunities for memorising, developing familiarity with different aspects of reading and experimenting for themselves by looking ahead:

> 16Fam: "My son was picking up some basic words like his brother did by being read to"
>
> 6F: "I pointed out common words or she decided to sound out some straight-forward words. She learnt to recognise more and more words as we read together."
>
> 33F: "Also reading to her directly as compared to listening to an audio book, although time consuming they watch the words and read ahead at times."
>
> 36Fam: "[he] figured out how to read at about 4 from looking at the words as we read the same stories over and over …"
>
> 62F: "The reading of many, many books to her when she could not speak and the fact that she took everything in while watching the pages."

These comments suggest a close proximity between children and the text being read to them and a concentration on the visual, as well as auditory, aspects of being read to. Parents clearly felt that they were giving children information about reading by reading to them in a particular physical form.

For other parents the importance of reading aloud was more greatly associated with the acquaintance it furthered with literary works and the knowledge and communicative practices that are associated with such acquaintance; in other words, the auditory aspects of being read to. These parents talked about reading aloud as part of the development of knowledge, vocabulary, expression and comprehension as well as encouraging a love of stories and literature:

> 32Fam: "Read TO THEM and let them continue to grow in knowledge by listening to stories on CD etc. Their comprehension will be great, and their language sophisticated by the time they start reading themselves."
>
> 19Fam: "My children [have been able] to listen to books they would not yet be able to read, thus improving their vocabulary and I think, increasing their later ability to figure out words as they read."
>
> 7Fam: "reading to kids helps develop a love of literature and vocabulary but doesn't speed reading along."
>
> 6F: "My part in her learning to read was reading with her FOR THE STORY."
>
> 4Fam "A love of books is the most important step. It doesn't matter if a child reads at 4 or 9, if they learn early that books are fascinating and love the experience of curling up and being read to, they will become passionate readers in their own good time."

These parents echo the view of Gordon Wells that "what is so important about listening to stories, then, is that through this experience, the child is beginning to discover the symbolic potential of language; its power to create possible or imaginary worlds through words" (Wells, 1986, p156). In turn this type of belief about reading aloud is likely to affect the nature of the material being read and the expected responses from the children being read to.

Which point of view parents took is capable of exerting a physical as well as mental and even emotional difference on the experience of being read to. For child and parent to see the book simultaneously a physical proximity is necessary which suggests a concentrated activity, perhaps with emotional closeness too, as children sit on laps or snuggle close next to the reader. Furthermore, if the intention behind the reading is to impart ideas about reading, a text may be selected with this in mind; perhaps one with fewer, shorter words and more illustrations. If the emphasis lies purely on the story however, parents and children could be further apart, listening to an audio version in the car or doing other things whilst they listened. Texts would more likely be selected with excitement or interest or amusement in mind. Of course this is not to say that families may not alter their style of reading aloud and their intentions over time or even from reading to reading. However, the point to make here is that being read to is not an homogenous experience and may be substantially altered according to the ideas and purposes behind it.

Reading aloud as participation

The previous chapter discussed the possibility of considering learning to read in terms of cultural participation rather than as the individual acquisition of a cognitive skill. In these terms, reading aloud to children can be seen as a participatory event in which the literacy lives of parents and children are formed and altered through their mutual intertwining. Being read to is not the mere experience of a passive child but is a mutually determined and determining event in which children and parents negotiate and share literacy lives in ways which shape new meaning and involvement for all:

> 41Fam: "At 6 she discovered 'Bratz'. I refused to read the books to her."
>
> 7Fam: "My family reads to him (we each have our own novel on the go and he roams from person to person begging

us to read). So he's doing *Lord of the Rings, Redwall,* The *Hobbit* and various Nancy Drews at the moment."

12F: "Reading aloud, parent reading to child, parents reading to one another and parents reading things aloud to themselves in the child's presence and later, child reading to parent or other child."

80M: "We still listen to many books on CD together and discuss what is happening." (11-year-old boy reading for past 3 years.)"

Reading habits may become self- reinforcing behaviours in which, for example, the parent reads, the child enjoys listening, so the parent reads more so that both parent and child are caught up in the same, mutually influencing literacy life:

36M: "He is still being read to. He enjoys that very much." (12-year-old boy reading for past two – three years.)"

Seeing reading aloud as a participation in a cultural practice or seeing the family as a community of literacy practice appears to be borne out by the number of families in which parents continued to read to children and teenagers whether or not those children could read for themselves:

15Fam: "The children are read to every night until the teen years or so."

5Fam: "I read regularly to my children from an early age until they were about 11 and 13."

3M: "We also still read to him – usually for 30 mins at night time." (son reading independently for several years.)

72M: "I still try to read to him on a daily basis, but he does a lot of independent reading during the day."

Some sort of educational intent is not precluded from the choice to continue family reading either as an explicit purpose or an incidental side effect:

28Fam: [I] "read to him, which I still try and do occasionally today. I just read him and his sister *Animal Farm* because I wanted us to discuss the book together."

However, many families simply stressed their pleasure in the practice:

19Fam "Reading out loud is still a major part of our family entertainment." (Two children both reading for several years)

5F: [I] "enjoyed reading to both children for years after they figured it out."

39Fam: "He was about 6 by the time he was reading by himself, though still loved being read to till about 16 when life for us all just got too busy."

Thinking about reading aloud, not as an educational function but as part of the ongoing practice of a literate community, as outlined in Lave and Wenger's model of the community of practice (1991), is able to incorporate the dynamic and changing nature of such an activity. For most children being read to was a long term habit or practice likely to have changed in character over the years. How and what they listened to and what children themselves enjoyed about or gained from the experience is likely to vary over the long term, as well as from child to child. Reading aloud as a family (i.e. to more than one child at the same time) instantly suggests a heterogeneous, non-standardised experience as participation, engagement and interest may well vary from child to child. Importantly in Lave and Wenger's model of communities of practice not all members of a given community will be having the same experience. Children growing up in the 'same' family and in the 'same' environment will still have unique experiences because of their unique positions within the family configuration as well as because of their own unique relationship to their literacy experiences.

What do children get out of being read to?

The most cited reason for reading aloud to children is that children will benefit educationally from the experience and will become better readers sooner for themselves (*Children Better Prepared For School If Their Parents Read Aloud to Them* (2008)). However, many children in this research read late in comparison with school age related norms. Even intensive being read to did not necessarily lead to early reading. Indeed, sometimes the opposite appeared to be so. For some children reading for themselves might appear pointless if they have a willing adult on hand to oblige:

> 4Fam: "Until then he was happy to be read to and couldn't see the point in learning to read."
>
> 43Fam: "I do not think they have been disadvantaged by not being able to read, because I have been there to facilitate their interaction with life and learning and to assist them by reading information for them as necessary."
>
> 78F: "She is a beginner reader and much prefers being read to"

That being read to might lessen motivation to read for oneself was born out by instances in which a parent's non-compliance with reading requests seems to have influenced a child into reading:

> 31Fam: "Well pretty soon he would want to read more so after the chapter when I was tired of reading or had something else to do, he would try to continue on his own."
>
> 2M: "He really took off with *Tintin*, which he used to pour over excessively and try to read, as I didn't like reading it much, so would only do a few pages at a time."

Or where a parent's reading aloud did not satisfactorily meet children's reading desires:

> 43F: "She had just barely enough skill to read Harry Potter so we read it together as above (as we had many times other books) and lo and behold, mom didn't read fast enough so my daughter started reading (voraciously) on her own."

> 53F: "My mother ... read to [me] every night, up to the age of about 8, when my reading skills overtook her reading speed."

Another factor which might influence habits of and pleasures taken in reading aloud at home is that of emotional settings. Every reading at home takes place in an emotional context adding an immeasurable dimension to the experience:

> 33F: "snuggling together also helps."

> 26M: "Reading was associated with parental attention, and hence had a positive impact on his development ... helping our boys to read through bedtime stories has only cemented our relationship."

> 33M: "If there were a particular genre [of preference] it would be funny books: ones that make him (and me his dad) laugh out loud."

> 11M: "I have taught 6 of my kids to read, I honestly think it was because it was with mama! We sit in bed and read and now the kids are big they still all read.

> 47M: "The focus of reading instruction really can be the reading of great books in a caring environment with people you love."

These insights into family literacy relationships contextualise children's own roles and influences, and therefore their own understandings of reading aloud. Reading at home is surrounded by relationships in which reciprocation and negotiation is motivated by circumstance and personal preferences and through which children's experiences of being read to are shaped. What is revealed are rich, deep relationships running through and around literacy lives and beyond. The consideration of these aspects and their impact on reading situations questions the straight forward correlation made between being read to and early reading in studies that concentrate purely on the 'educational' aspects of the situation.

How often children are read to

For some being read to was a way of life:

> 34Fam: "We just read to him what he wanted us to read to him."
>
> 36Fam: "We read several hours every day."
>
> 22Fam: "We just read aloud all the time everywhere: in bed, before breakfast, at meals, on the beach, in bed."
>
> 7Fam: "we read to the kids constantly."
>
> 3F: "Read and read and read to them."

For others it was a rare occurrence:

> 23Fam: "He has never let me read to him, and still does not want me to – he would rather read for himself!"
>
> 20Fam: "the youngest one ... never loved to be read stories to. He just loved to watch pictures with me and look for special things in the picture, but as soon as I started to read to him he was not interested."
>
> 1F: "[I] very rarely read to her ... she's never been into that, but lots of time just hanging out with her, laughing, playing etc... the pressure to read to your child for 10 minutes every night is aimed more at time-poor parents whose children have been away from them all day."
>
> 13F: "[she] never wanted to be read to as a child."

Some families attributed their children's disinterest in being read to, to negative experiences in school:

> 16Fam: "I think the issues he had at school with reading did a lot of damage to his enjoyment of books. He loved to sit and listen to stories and now won't do that."
>
> 66M: "He loved having stories read to him until he went to school, then he began to hate reading. Now he has gained a lot of interest back."

For other families no explanation came readily to mind:

> 13F: "[she] just wasn't interested in the world or books. She hated the fact that my house was full of books and interesting resources."

Within the research cohort the group of children who did not want to be read to was small but their experiences are particularly interesting. Of the six children who did not enjoy being read to, five had begun to read for themselves between the ages of three and a half and 10, one child aged 9 at the time of the questionnaire was not reading. The ages at which the five children began reading are unexceptional across the age spread in the rest of the sample. Similarly, the 9-year-old boy not yet reading is in no way remarkable compared to the rest of the cohort but it might be pertinent to add that he had been in school for 18 months where he had been identified as being in need of extra help and put on a reading programme. This group opens up a host of questions about the relationship of children's agency to the experiences of reading. These children are rejecting conventional good practice/wisdom in favour of their own autonomous reaction. Instead of receiving conventional experiences their situation is empowering their non-conformity. It is an unanswered question as to how this may affect their reading and/or other aspects of their education. However, like the children who rejected direct teaching, this group do not appear (within the limits of this research) to have been disadvantaged in anyway by their decision.

Dynamic situations

There are enough apparent differences emerging from accounts of reading aloud to children to question that the children being read to are all subject to the same experience all, or indeed any, of the time. Reading to children can take many forms and may take place in physical, intellectual and emotional contexts which vary to such extents between families, between children and over time that to call them the same thing may be very misleading. 'Reading aloud' cannot be assumed monolithically to mean the same or to make the same contribution to a child's literacy life, all of the time. This poses a problem for the deficit arguments of those like Gordon Wells who has argued that if children are not read to there will be particular detrimental consequences to their reading education (Wells 1986). From the examples of the home educating families and the apparent differences in the ways in which children are read to it is not adequate to simply say that being read to is missing in any particular case, where being read to has not been more carefully defined.

Instead, from the evidence presented here, reading aloud to children can be seen as a highly flexible, changeable, individual practice subject to all manner of variations, which is itself entering a relationship with a highly varied and changeable, individual subject; the child who is being read to.

Talking

Talk was the second most frequently mentioned influence on reading. Like reading aloud, talk is also considered a major influencing factor on reading in mainstream theory and the intertwining of language and literacy is commonplace in discussions of learning to read. The view of Britton that "reading and writing float on a sea of talk" (Britton, 1983, p. 11) is one which underlies much of our understanding of literacy. Sugata Mitra's experiments; placing a computer with internet connection into a wall in a Delhi slum district and watching the local children become acquainted with its functioning, however, offers an interesting antidote to this assumption. Mitra found that children who could not read or write in any language and who spoke no English became functionally literate on the computer unaided and "very fast" (Dhillon, 2013, p91).

If reading aloud is a theme too large and differentiated to be treated as a single monolithic influence, then talk certainly presents this problem. As with reading aloud, differing intentions as well as differing physical, intellectual and emotional contexts confounded by temporal and individual factors, as well as, of course, the varying nature of the talk itself, mean that it cannot possibly be satisfactorily subsumed under a general heading. Instead, as with reading aloud, we might approach talk in a very general way through the means of its perceived contribution to learning to read.

Talk as a form of transmission

Talk was sometimes referred to as a direct contributor to reading in the sense that talk was used as a vehicle for transmitting information about reading:

> 16F: "talking about letter sounds occasionally."
>
> 24F: "I would also chat about words e.g. If you substitute B for the C you get BAT. But it was all conversational."
>
> 33M: "We employ conversational learning on an ad hoc basis e.g. Driving past an Asda store we will point out and say 'A for Asda'."
>
> 72M: "We also talked about the sounds that the letters make, and he seemed to grasp this concept easily."

Answering children's questions

One particular kind of talk which transmitted information like this was answering children's questions; a factor cited by Margaret Clark (1976) as critical in the children whom she studied who had learned to read without being taught prior to beginning school. As discussed in the previous chapter, children were frequently pro-active, seeking out what they needed to pursue in their literacy lives and chief amongst their resources were their parents. For their part parents placed significant emphasis on their roles in answering and being available to answer children's questions:

> 44Fam: "The majority of this conveyance was in response to their questions or by way of follow up comment."
>
> 31Fam: "Answering their questions was the factor that helped them the most."
>
> 23Fam: "We are available to answer any questions AS THEY

HAPPEN!"

21Fam: "We always encourage questions and never fob them off when we answer."

20Fam: "Of course we answered their questions."

12Fam: "We ALWAYS answered our daughters when they asked what something said and how/why."

The importance placed on answering questions, rather than initiating teaching, connects to the perception of children as individual learners and to the principles of child-led and paced learning. Answering children's questions is a way of following children's interests into literacy as opposed to teacher initiated information which will possibly lead learning in a direction which is not meaningful or relevant to its recipient:

50M: "I don't need to teach him, just be there to answer his questions and be guided by him."

The strategy of answering children's questions often led to what might appear to be a reduction in transmitted material in that what children frequently wanted was not theories to help them read but simply to have something read for them:

21F: "When she started reading on her own she would ask us when she didn't know a word."

36F: "Answering the 'does that say?' type questions."

40M: "When reading on his own if he doesn't know a word he asks what it was, and I tell him."

59F: "Willingness to answer 'what's this word?' very, very frequently."

62F: "We also used to go into town and she would ask the name of every shop and what things said."

Knowing what things say, rather than receiving information about reading theories, may be more helpful in children organising their own understanding even if sometimes it could feel like a missed opportunity for a lesson:

24F: "[I] only answered questions truthfully. So if she asked "how do I spell cat?" I would tell her immediately. I didn't ask her to work it out for herself."

46M: "[we] always directly answered his questions. We NEVER said 'look it up' unless it was in the sentence 'I don't know, I'll have to look it up and get back to you.'"

81M: "Sometimes it means asking mom and dad 'What does xyz spell?' (just answer him! Don't turn it into a lesson)."

Whilst the chance to give an impromptu lesson may be hard to turn down, from a participation rather than an acquisition point of view a literacy situation has been enabled. An adult reading instructions to a child which then allows the child to go ahead with, for example, a computer game or building a model, has enabled participation in a literacy experience. This is quite distinct from the adult who uses the opportunity to further a theory on reading by asking a child, for example, to sound out the words for him or herself.

Chapter Three discussed the role of theories such as phonics in learning to read. Answering children's questions is a good way of understanding how much and what these theories mean to them. Some children's questions showed that they were linking their ideas about reading to these adult theories as many questions about reading were framed within recognisable main stream propositions:

4M: "Told him what the letters sounded like when he asked."

58F: "just answering questions about letters and their sound."

30M: "Following his lead when he wanted to know the NAMES and sounds of letters and sounds of groups of letters."

Whilst at other times the source of questions could appear more obscure:

65M: "Answer their questions even if they appear strange."

In the cases where it is hard to know why a child is asking

particular things, by simply giving the requested information parents were allowing the mental space in which children could explore and test their own theories. In addition, simply supplying the answer enables children to get on with their participation in the literacy event of the moment.

Talk as participation

Talk was also viewed much more generally as contributing to reading, in the sense of enhancing vocabulary, expression, experiencing different types of communication, using words in ways that would eventually cross over into reading although not necessarily in any purposeful or direct way:

> 44Fam: "Responsive, interactive parenting: lots of conversation"

> 22Fam: "Lots of conversation"

> 2F: "Communication. Talking, laughing, listening, singing. We did not use 'baby talk' but always spoke to her normally and respectfully and we accepted her communication no matter how unintelligible it was."

> 45M: "In our daily errands he would ask questions. We would talk about the signs we saw. How the Target store has a target for a bull's-eye, how the STOP signs are red hexagons, etc. Just regular conversations."

> 43Fam: "Always being available (as much as possible, that is!) to answer questions, play a game, talk, speculate, read a book …"

The kind of talk described above can also be seen as an element of participation in family and cultural, as well as literacy life. Talk at home can be quite different from talk in school as Tizard and Hughes' comparative study of young girls' conversations at home and at nursery school shows (Tizard and Hughes, 1984). One of the main features that distinguish what they describe as the quality of talk in the different settings is that the mothers at home share the child's world and can thus extend the conversation over time, linking the immediate to the past and future as well as being able to refer to a breadth of subject matter through their knowledge of their children's experiences. This kind of talk is much more integrated into the rest of life including its links to literacy experiences.

Talk as an on-going feature of life; the long discussions and conversations, as the idea of hours and hours spent reading aloud, speak again of the wider home education relationships and context in which parents and children are each other's constant and intimate companions.

> 53M: "On long journeys we listen to the national radio station and have long discussions about a range of topics, or listen to audio books. At night over dinner we again have discussions about current issues in the news, ideas and thoughts. ... all in all words whether written or spoken are a huge part of his life."

Talk about reading could be seen as a facet of this rather than as being solely concerned with its educative aspects:

> 15Fam: "We talk about books."
>
> 45Fam: "She enjoys being able to discuss books with the family too."

Games/toys/ computers

A third influencing factor brought up by parents was that of games and recreational activities including the use of computers, electronic games and watching television. The type of games and activities mentioned ranged from simple oral word games like 'I spy' to sophisticated on line games such as World of Warcraft. Again the question arises as to why such a diverse range of activities should be put together as a 'theme' that might help explain how children learn to read. One possible reason is that such games contain information about reading: phonics, words and letters which is easily transmitted and practiced through the playing of enjoyable games:

> 36Fam: "I also played many games with letters and sounds and words and shared how letters and sounds work"

> 32Fam: "Played games like BINGO for letters and word recognition, played "concentration" card game, matching words, saying them as we found them etc ... We also used Leap Frog where the child can point the electronic pencil at the word, and the book pronounced the word."

> 29Fam: "We ... played some games like writing letters and groups of letters on blocks and letting him match them together to make words. We also played matching games – I'd write words on index cards and draw pictures of the words on other cards and he'd match them up."

> 8F: "We also have some flashcards and have played 'word hide and seek' with them as she learnt to recognise the words."

> 62M: "Using foam letters in the bathtub to make words and learn the alphabet."

> 77M: "Phonics games played on the computer."

Presenting material in this way can make transmission fun and easy:

> 54F: "Best treated as just another game/daily experience ... I was astonished for instance, at how quickly my daughter learnt to recognise all the letters when she was interested and saw it as an exciting game."

However, some parents added remarks that distanced them from the idea that these games should be seen in terms of an input into a learning process, whilst others did not mention this possible aspect at all. Instead they emphasised the immediate fun and voluntary nature of the activities; a scenario more akin to a group of friends playing cards where an understanding of what is happening would likely be based on enjoyment, shared activity and companionship rather than seeing the game as a vehicle for the transmission of information about its content.

> 68M: "He enjoys playing with letter fridge magnets, entirely if and when he chooses."
>
> 24F: "We would doodle on paper messing around with the letters to make new words."
>
> 2F: "We also play board games as a family.... We (as a family) love words, play around with them, love rhyme and nonsense words (and the sounds they make)."
>
> 14Fam: "We played a lot of games such as I spy and letter jigsaws etc."
>
> 45F: "We had things like reading and spelling games around, but she's never really enjoyed them, except that it was a chance to hang out with the person playing the game with her."

The intention with which these activities are viewed becomes the crucial factor in deciding what is happening in the playing of these games. Games can be seen as a means of transmitting information related to reading but if reading is seen as a cultural activity in which children are gradually becoming active participants then there is nothing to transmit. Instead the purpose of the activity is solely involvement in it. Some parents explicitly acknowledged that what they were seen to be doing and what they intended might be open to conflicting interpretation. This point was made in Chapter Four in relation to the discussion on teaching. What makes the crucial difference is not what actions are being taken but how those actions are interpreted.

> 38F: "We did play a lot of games that involved recognising and matching words not with the intention of her learning anything from them."

For these parents, the concern seems to have been the spontaneous fun provided by the game rather than the transmission of educational content. Of course this could be interpreted quite differently by an outside observer.

Children's play and other interests

Children themselves seem to spontaneously play with words and reading for two reasons; the intrinsic and the instrumental. Especially very young children found intrinsic interest and pleasure in sounds and instruments like computer keyboards:

> 48M: "Very early interest in playing with sounds (2 years old)."

> 39F: "At 18 months she taught herself the alphabet by pressing letters on the computer."

Or children might be interested in what reading and writing can bring to a situation:

> 67M: "He chooses when he wants to write signs for his play games."

That reading could instrumentally enhance the enjoyment of some games and play activities seems to have acted as a spur to reading for some children:

> 73M: "I feel ... the need to read even for such things as Play Station games did the job for me."

> 10M: "He learned ultimately by collecting and playing Yugioh and Pokemon cards."

> 64M: "His brothers and sister had several Pokemon games on their GBAs. He was a big Pokemon fan and soon realised that he needed to be able to read in order to play the games himself. He learnt very quickly."

> 81M: "He needed to find a reason to want to read. We started playing World of Warcraft and he found his reason."

> 20M: "He was very eager to find free online games on the computer. He would ask me how to spell "free" "online" "games" and it was through this interest that he started reading."

> 41Fam: "Playing on her DS Lite has also encouraged her to read by having many game instructions as text."

> 20Fam: "both read anything on the computer they love for example World of Warcraft and anything to do with the game."
>
> 17M: "He wanted to read to play his Gameboy games."
>
> 28M: "wanting to read cheats for computer games."
>
> 32M: "He learnt a year or so later because of a Pokemon game on the Gameboy. There was quite a bit of reading on each screen and I think he got fed up of having to continually ask a member of the family to read it to him so worked it out himself."

There could also be a social aspect to engaging in literacy practices as a form of communication:

> 6Fam: "For my daughter, she is in love with her texting cell phone and laptop. All her friends read, email and text. She wants to be part of that."

Again, these examples can be understood in terms of gradual participation in family and group activities. A young child pressing computer keys or making noises for fun can be seen as imitating what he or she has heard and seen others doing. Children joining in family entertainment or playing popular games such as World of Warcraft and Pokemon can also be seen as participating in community and cultural activities. The motivation which appears to spur on this participation however is not necessarily a motivation to read per se. Instead children are motivated to pursue a particular activity (the game) and in doing so incidentally participate in reading (Thomas and Pattison 2007).

One aspect of engaging in this type of literacy activity is that the written material being used has not been prepared with learning to read in mind. Conventional beginner reading material is carefully designed and specifically graded. It can stand in stark contrast to the kind of literacy found on, for example, Pokemon cards which as Gee (2009) points out are written in specialist language the equivalent of which children are not likely to meet in school for several years; "in fact, in complexity, it is far above the language many young children see in their schoolbooks until they get to middle school at best and, perhaps, even high school" (Gee, 2009, p 317). However, as many parents testified, this did not appear to prevent children from engaging with it.

Television

Some parents mentioned the influence of television, particularly that with sub-titles:

> 11M: "closed captioning on the TV (or telly to you folks in the UK)."
>
> 17M: "We watched 'Between the Lions' together, had closed captioning on the television all the time."
>
> 41F: "She chose to put on the subtitles whenever she watched TV."
>
> 24M: "He learned to read from playing video games where the characters' speech was subtitled."
>
> 35M: "He watched some "educational" TV that used phonics. (We consider all TV to be educational.) … in addition he is playing video games where reading is helpful and he is motivated."
>
> 63M: "He worked it out for himself by watching words as we read to him and reading the subtitles on the TV."

For some however, the influence of the screen was not seen as positive:

> 13Fam: "They didn't watch screens."
>
> 33F: "I've a feeling that restricting media has helped the focus on reading as entertainment and fascination for what's in books and wanted to read for themselves."
>
> 39F: "We don't have a TV so we all read a lot."
>
> 9M: "He did not watch TV – reading was the main entertainment in our house."

The mixed views on television, as was the case with the children who did not enjoy being read to, illustrates again the difficulties of constructing a deficit argument in which certain criteria may be considered as essential 'inputs' which can then be identified as missing in other examples. These differing experiences suggest that what may be considered helpful to one child should not be extended to be considered missing for another child.

The differing views on television illustrate parents' point that learning is individual and what suits one child may not suit another. By extension this also forms an argument against the idea of method altogether. Children are able to put together for themselves, from what is available around them, information and connections sufficiently to create and sustain meaning that is applicable to their worlds. Most theories of reading centre around certain things – experiences, bits of knowledge, personal attributes and abilities – which are deemed essential to reading. If one or more is missing, or is weak, then children will not learn successfully. However, this research suggests that there is no essential core that all children must have; rather that there are multiple possibilities and combinations as opposed to narrow necessities. Instead what comes over is again the diversity and individuality of children's literacy experiences at home. It is these differences rather than the similarities in experiences between families and indeed within families that seem key in understanding learning to read. This idea will be returned to in the final chapter.

Chapter Six

Learning trajectories

Learning anything in our society is generally seen as being a matter of progressive improvement over time. Practice, teaching, and experience are all mapped onto a timeline of improvement, 'the learning curve' of common parlance. This chapter explores some of the ideas behind this common way of understanding learning and looks at how experiences at home sometimes contradict this widespread perception.

Reading trajectories

In main stream education learning to read is generally portrayed as a series of stages. Each of these stages is to do with assembling sub parts that will eventually contribute to the overall skill of reading. These sub parts begin with 'pre-reading skills' such as phonemic awareness, eye - brain coordination, language development, concentration, left to right orientation and so on. From there children go on to learn decoding beginning with short, phonetic words and progressing to longer words and texts and gradually towards non-phonetic words. Teaching programmes like the Oxford Reading Tree are especially written to walk children through this process; consolidating skills and taking them on to the next level. Learning to read, or resolving problems in learning to read, is treated as a matter of ensuring that the various levels of skills are all addressed and sufficiently developed. Assessment in reading consists of testing children to see if they can complete various tasks that represent these skills. Such testing can actually take place away from reading, beginning before a child can read with the assessment of pre-reading skills and working through to the ability to read words and sentences that have been judged increasingly 'difficult' (Torgeson, 1998). This view of reading as a linear development has been turned into a standardised way of thinking about how the child of learning theories or a 'normal' child learns to read.

Figure 2 shows what has come to be considered as a standard reading trajectory. Over time the learner progresses from beginner to advanced level in a smooth upward curve. This simple idea has immense power in our education system and indeed has come to dominate our cultural understandings of not just reading but learning in general. When children learn to read in school their learning is attached to an expected trajectory. It is this curve that lies behind the age/ability expectations through which progress is assessed and is the kind of thinking behind such statements as that of Schools' Minister Nick Gibb in 2011,

"There is no doubt we need to raise standards of reading. Only last month we learnt that one in 10 boys aged 11 can read no better than a seven-year-old."

(Nick Gibb reported by Harrison (2011)).

Clearly this statement is based on an envisaged trajectory such as the one below in which the child's age can be located on the time line and her or his expected ability in reading then read off the curve to assess his or her progress. Similarly, if a child of a given age is not reaching the point on the curve in line with their current age then he or she is late (or early) in reading.

Standard reading trajectory

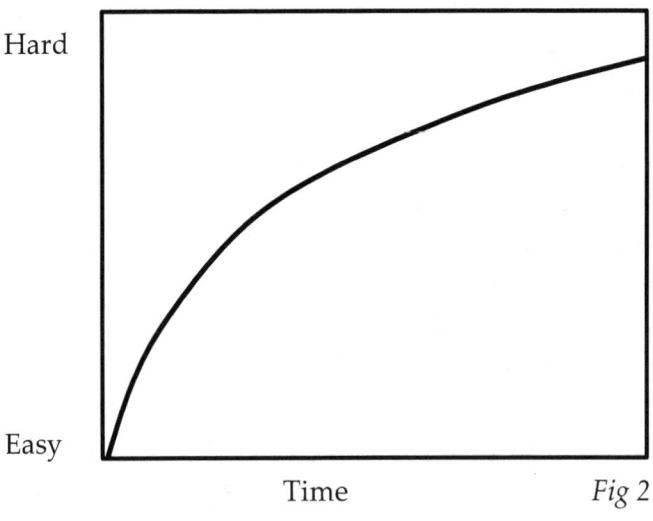

Fig 2

For some families learning did follow more or less the same path as this expected formal trajectory, although learning trajectories did not necessarily relate to age designations in the same way. In fact a great deal of flexibility regarding age was apparent even when children appeared to be following this familiar course of learning:

> 11Fam, "They began by learning letter names and sounds ... then we moved on to using wooden building blocks to spell common, easy words ... Eventually we began getting 10 word readers from the library ..."

Others described a build-up but with less specific detail:

> 78M: "basic reading about 6 or 7, but really reading well at 8"

> 44Fam: "3-4 for simple words, 5-6 for things like the first Harry Potter, although more like 6 – 7 for really fluent reading of more difficult material."

However, this was not always the experience. For one thing, the trajectory was not always a smooth one. Sometimes learning seemed to come in fits and starts:

Incremental incline

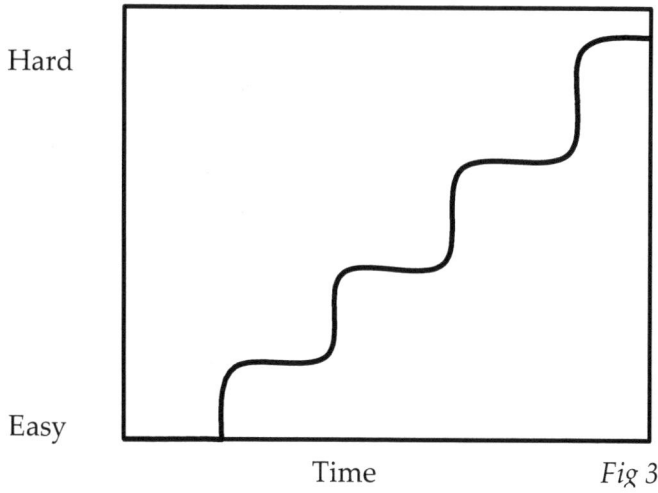

Fig 3

> T14Fam: "Learning to read is not necessarily a linear, gradual process. As with all learning, it has its plateaux and its

spurts."

T12F: "I found it very interesting that it seemed to go in big jumps rather than a gradual progression. She had all the basics (knowledge of letters, sounds) at 18 months but no interest in reading. At 2.5 she wanted to read the basic readers but didn't make progress beyond that for about 9 months and then a sudden light went on and she was able to read 3rd grade chapter books and swiftly (within another few months) things like *Charlotte's Web*."

8M: "He recognised words from about the age of 5 but showed no interest in reading until he was 10 when he suddenly stopped asking us to read his Beano as he wanted to do it for himself."

Sometimes the fits and starts manifested in long breaks, often of years in duration, in which reading did not appear on children's agendas. Yet this did not necessarily mean that children's abilities were stagnating. One parent discussed her thoughts on the lack of continuity in learning trajectories:

32 Fam: "The process was not continuous. There was a week or some weeks when reading and writing or the interest on the subject was very intense and then there was no interest for weeks or months. But when they started to be interested again I always noticed that there has been something happening in between ... after a while they made connections which they didn't do before or there was just more knowledge than before."

In other examples children who had been being taught hit a difficulty, stopped reading as a result only to find when they came back to it that the problem had disappeared:

3Fam: "I actually only taught him the technique up to a point. We hit a brick wall with words that had more than 2 syllables and so I left it, only to discover that he started reading long words by himself a month later."

From these experiences it seems that breaks, time 'off task' to use the school speak, can actually offer a valuable contribution to learning. This is an interesting point when compared to the annual concern that children 'go backwards' during the course of long summer holidays; a phenomenon which has been particularly noted amongst families lower down the socio-economic scale as they are found less likely to engage in approved literacy practices during the break (Jesson et al, 2014).

Downward curve learning

On the standardised trajectory we expect children to begin with material designated easy and progress to material designated hard. Reading schemes lay out texts in this way and it seems so much of a common sense that it is rarely questioned that this should be the obvious way to go about learning. However, some parents reported quite different experiences:

> 16Fam: "We now find that he can read words such as 'escape', 'organic', 'save', 'exit', 'bungalow', 'dinosaur', 'bytes' but struggles with the traditional phonic words 'cat', 'hat', 'bit' which I find totally fascinating that he retains the words he needs to be able to do the things he wants to do but doesn't retain the words that are of no interest to him."

> 28Fam: "He also really enjoyed the Flanimals books by Ricky Gervais and could read words like 'underblenge' before things we would consider simple."

> 22F: "She is the posterchild for asynchronous learning, with understanding of higher concepts occurring before basic 'foundation' skills in almost all areas of learning for her."

For children like these the standard learning trajectory seems to have been reversed as they apparently begin with 'difficult' words and 'harder' concepts before accomplishing the usually designated easy material.

Downward curve

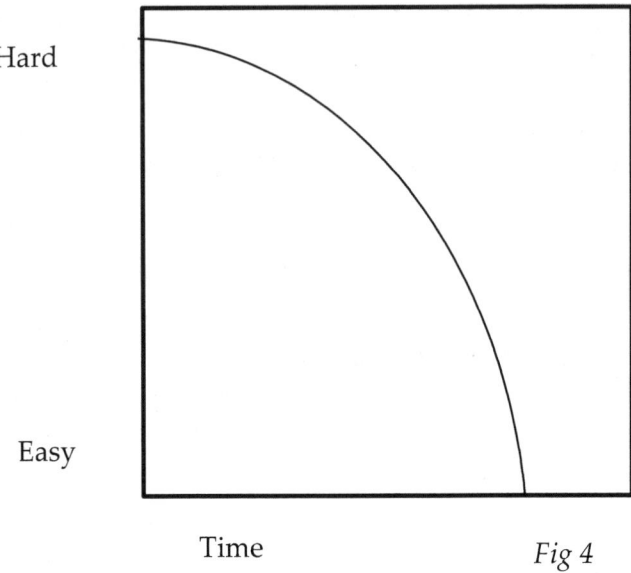

Fig 4

Part of what colours our view here is the designations of 'hard' and 'easy'. In reading this is nearly always aligned to phonics. Words that are short and follow the rules of phonics like 'cat', 'shop' or 'red' are easy; words that are long and don't follow the rules are hard: 'dough', 'conscious', 'bristle'. Some children in the sample did learn to read using phonics but for many phonics appeared to play little or no part. For this second group the phonetic designations of 'hard' and 'easy' would be meaningless. Instead we need to consider other reasons why children might be attracted to some words or find them easy to read. Such reasons could include that the word is particularly meaningful to them; many children learn to recognize their own names very early on because this is perhaps the most personally significant word to them. There can also be other words which children might recognize because they are very common; children see them frequently and become familiar with them:

> 22F: "I remember laughing that she recognized the word 'loading' which she'd learnt by looking at it while

waiting for various games to load up!"

Another reason why children might be attracted to certain words or texts is simply that they have a wider reason to be interested in them. This last point came up again and again. It seems that it wasn't so much where children started (in terms of difficulty) but with what they started (in terms of interest) that mattered. And in this, parents saw subject appeal as paramount:

> 22F: "having something that really truly interests the person is really important. Even (perhaps especially) if it's far beyond their reading 'level'."
>
> 23M: "I think the main thing is to allow them to read whatever they are interested in, even if the topic or book seems 'too hard' for their level."
>
> T6F: "Reading interest started with serious books way above her 'level'. Christopher Paolini's series beginning with Eldest and formula horse novelettes (following her interest, not her reading level)."

When children knew what they wanted to read and went straight to those texts the linear progression of 'easy' to 'hard' appeared immaterial:

> 23M: "He largely taught himself to read from field guides (he loves nature)."
>
> 64M: "He was a big Pokemon fan and soon realised that he needed to be able to read in order to play the games himself. He learnt very quickly."

It may be the case that when children are interested in a text they look at it differently to texts that don't excite them. It may also be that particular interest can generate its own method of learning. Children might learn a favourite book by heart and then transfer the recognition of words in one context to words in another.

> 32M: "We'd always read out loud to him and he knew some books by heart word for word so I wonder if that helped him work out the code of reading but don't really know."

This is a method usually frowned on in formal education where children are required to use phonetic methods only to sound out words and where learning through memorisation is avoided even to the extent that made up nonsense words are used on reading tests (as are currently used in the UK see Department of Education 2016). At home however, and as discussed in Chapter Three, it seems that memorisation can be an effective strategy, at least for some children.

The downward curve questions the assertion of an objective starting point in learning to read. Across the data the children who had begun reading with an interest in surprisingly advanced, non-beginner texts had no common starting point. The texts might all be 'difficult' but apart from that they were all different. The standardized learning trajectory postulates a foundational basis for beginning reading but the experiences of the downward curve readers illustrates how restrictive this kind of thinking can be. Across the range of home educating experiences, it would be impossible to standardize a starting point and this in itself suggests a far wider variation in learning to read than is generally taken into account.

Non-progressive learning

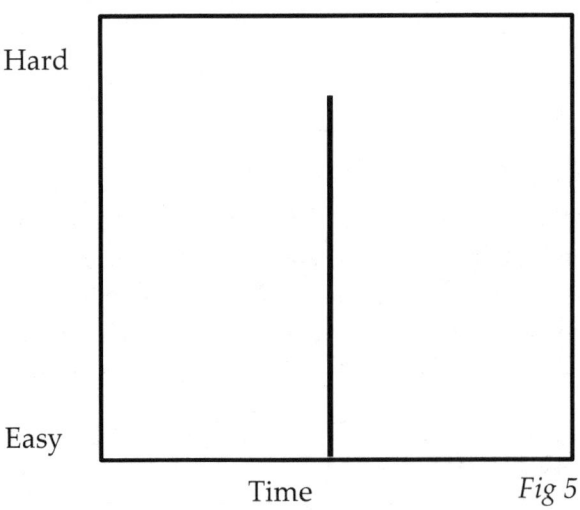

Fig 5

Closely allied to downward curve learning is what might be considered as non-progressive learning. For some children a progression into reading seemed impossible to trace. They appeared to learn very quickly and to go from being non-readers to reading whatever they liked without a discernible learning trajectory at all.

> 2Fam: "Not sure how he learnt to read – seemed to happen overnight!"
>
> 36 Fam: "Then, quite abruptly, or so it seemed to me, she began to read independently. She moved from deciphering very simple board books to being able to read absolutely anything - aloud, with different voices for different characters - in about two months."
>
> 37Fam: "Both read it [*The Lord of the Rings*] within months of 'clicking' with reading."
>
> 30M: "He went from reading a few words to reading something 200 pages plus in less than a year."

This kind of sudden burst into reading was often described through dramatic metaphors like light bulbs flashing on, or switches being thrown.

> 62F: "She suddenly launched into reading by herself."
>
> 46F: "Then a sudden light went on and she was able to read 3rd grade chapter books and swiftly (within another few months) things like *Charlotte's Web*."
>
> 1M: "It was as though a switch was thrown."

Two possible ways of rationalising these dramatic experiences were talked about by parents. Some parents speculated that reading rather than being the attainment of a certain point on a given trajectory gained through the incremental build-up of sub-parts is a much more amorphous process consisting of a coming together in the mind:

> 14F: "Becoming a reader is a mystery that happens when several things coalesce in the brain."

> 32 Fam: "Like a dough with yeast which is going up and you don't have to do anything than mixing the right ingredients. It was a bit like mixing the right ingredients (but not myself has been the one who knew those)."

Rather than reading building up through a step by step process these comments suggest that it is a fusion of elements that amalgamate in the mind; a rather different metaphor to that of building skills and one that has deep implications for how we think about learning. The mother in the last quote distances herself further from the building skills approach in her comment that she does not know what the elements of reading are. Again this is a very important point which has profound repercussions for re-thinking learning to read and one that will be returned to later.

A second possibility is that whilst these examples do not follow a conventional path that does not necessarily mean that there is no progressive movement into reading. It might simply be that the progress we culturally expect to see is not always the important one which allows reading to happen. As one parent put it:

> 8M: "One of the biggest problems of school is that it makes the children demonstrate and show off intermediate skills that might not be good for learning the final skill for some children."

For some children at least it may be that other things, things which current theories do not consider, are what matter more in learning to read.

The standardised learning trajectory, the easy to hard progression over time, has been very influential in homogenising our thinking about reading. The evidence from the home educating families shows that this is not the only way and that there is still much to be explored in thinking about how children learn to read.

What's happening in non-linear, non-progressive learning?

The standard learning trajectory curve makes a number of assumptions about learning to read which have become incorporated into educational thinking to the point that they are very rarely questioned. These assumptions are that children will begin reading from a common starting point, that they will progress at a standard rate, that learning is a continuous process, that reading is a skill consisting of other skills and can be broken down into these parts for the purpose of learning. The evidence from the home educating families however, calls these assumptions into question.

The data here suggests that there are possible learning trajectories that current reading theories do not account for. We know from other countries such as Finland that children who begin the taught process at a later age learn to read very successfully and overtake British children in competence according to international comparisons like Pisa (Antikainen 2007). Other reading trajectories are therefore possible; but in the UK at least, they are also largely unexplored. Rather than home educators feeling that they must explain their children's deviance from the standard trajectory or have that trajectory imposed on them, the evidence from children educated at home demands the re-thinking of normalised courses to account for much higher degrees of variability and idiosyncrasy than has been the case up until now. Our new understanding of learning to read may look much more like the deliberately unlabelled figure 6 aptly described by this parent:

> 22F: "The process is a complicated series of leaps and halts, progressions and regressions of a non-linear nature".

Fig 6

Chapter Seven

Assessment and 'late' reading

"How do you know they are learning?", "Are they meeting their targets?", "Do you test them?", "Still not reading? There might be genuine problems". Assessing learning is part and parcel of our education system so much so that it is often spoken about as if it is an essential part of all education. Home educators are often asked about assessment in the kinds of questions listed above and parents too can agonise over how much they need to keep track of learning and how best to do so. Assessment however, is not something that stands alone; it is closely bound to how we understand what learning is and particularly how we perceive paths of learning to develop. This chapter looks at how learning to read unfolds at home and the kinds of questions this raises about reading assessment.

Assessment

Assessment, as it is used in main stream schooling, aims to measure learning and to act as a means of predicting and improving learning along a given trajectory. For it to do its job that trajectory of learning needs to be pre-decided so that children's progress along it can be measured. The evidence from this research suggests that learning to read at home does not necessarily follow any such trajectory, on the contrary, the preceding chapter has highlighted how varied learning to read at home can be. Children learn on different and unpredictable time scales, they do not learn at uniform rates, some at least do not learn in the kind of sequence that has come to be seen as logical. Given this, learning to read at home cannot be effectively assessed by the usual method of relating individual children to pre-determined age/ability targets. Nor is the orthodox notion of progress along the standard reading trajectory able to encompass or explain the wide range of cases documented here. Equally, the same pressures to measure learning in school do not exist at home. Many parents viewed assessment as something rather different and many perhaps would not even think in terms of quantifying learning. This, however, did not mean that parents were not interested in their children's learning or were not curious, and sometimes anxious, about their accomplishments.

The research questionnaire did not directly ask parents about assessment but the matter did lie implicitly in some of the questions. For instance, parents were asked at what age they would say their child became able to read. In order to answer this question parents had to make some kind of assessment of their child's reading ability.

How do you know when they are reading?

In mainstream education this is a question which would perhaps raise eyebrows if not be outrightly laughable. We know what children can do because they are regularly tested and those tests will place them at a particular level within the framework of learning to read; so we don't just know that they can read but we also know how well. But away from this regime how a parent can tell when a child is reading becomes a much more nebulous, subjective, and generally more difficult question. When parents were asked at what age their children had learned to read they replied with a spread of answers between 18 months and 16 years yet it was also clear that, for many, there was more to this question than a simple number.

Many parents were uncertain about when their child had started reading. This could be for a number of reasons: because they saw learning to read as a progress that takes place over a number of years, because the child had learned autonomously and parents had become aware that they could read rather than following their progress, because they had read different things at different ages for example signs at 6, books at 11, and a couple of parents said that they suspected that their children had probably been reading before they could speak.

Some parents commented on the progression of ability from beginner to fully fledged reader:

5M: "read 3 ½, read well 4"

59F: "ages 6 ½ (beginning) to 9 (confident)"

43F: "8 years, but basics at 3 yrs"

Some parents differentiated between the material children read:

28F: "4 – quite a few words, 5 – anything"

30F "Posters and signs from 5 years but wouldn't read a book until 8"

44Fam: "3-4 for simple words, 5-6 for things like the first Harry Potter, although more like 6 – 7 for really fluent reading of more difficult material."

18F: "She could read CVC words by age 3, but wasn't reading full books independently until 5 or 6. So it's hard to pick one age."

12Fam: "5 (novels at 8)."

43M: "Logos – 18 months, books – 5"

62M: "words 2 – 3, books 4 – 5"

Both these types of answers suggested that parents were talking about a progressive process which they were able to trace. Other parents gave an impression of general uncertainty about the question:

28Fam: "around five,"

79M: "5 or 6"

16M: "6 or 7"

46M: "11 or 12. Don't recall exactly."

29M "he became fluent at about 8 – 9 years."

2F: "Not sure, but she was young."

8M: "Not sure"

Where children are learning autonomously with only minimal, intermittent or no direct parental input parents are unsurprisingly somewhat detached from the process and therefore less likely to be able to put a specific age on an accomplishment moment. Parents then discover that their child is reading but may have had no sense of any build up process before this point and therefore cannot say for how long their child has been reading:

- 1M: "It was fascinating to observe him decoding the mechanics of the written word (once I was aware he was doing it!)"
- 32M: "We weren't really aware that he had [started to read] until he started reading the TV schedule in broadsheet newspapers which made us think he was fairly fluent. This would have been about 8 years old I think, maybe 9."

Oher parents found the idea of even informal assessment intrusive and some children preferred to be left alone:

- 59M: "We don't know and don't want to ask how much he can actually read, but we're sure he's learning."
- 38F: "We know now that she was doing a lot of reading in secret … When she was about five, we realised she was a pretty fluent reader."
- 11Fam: "I find that my son does better when I pretend that I'm not looking or listening too much (he gets self-conscious otherwise.)"

On the other hand, parents and children in home education tend to live very closely and have ample opportunities to come to know what is going on in each other's lives. As one parent put it:

- 45M: "I began to suspect that he was beginning to read on his own due to various reasons."

Common place, day to day interaction can be very revealing about what children are doing and how they feel about what they are doing. There seemed to be three main ways in which parents knew whether and how much their children were reading. These ways were not used as assessment strategies in the sense of parents deliberately setting out to find out where their children were at, instead this knowledge emerged from ordinary interaction between parents and children. It was not something that parents had to go seeking for.

Demonstration

Sometimes children spontaneously demonstrated what they could do either in a deliberate fashion or casually as part of something else that they were doing.

>5Fam: "At 3 ½ he was reading me the labels on the cross section of a fish at Bristol zoo."

>5Fam: "He came to me one day 'look Mum I can read this word,' then 'look mum I can read this sentence,' then 'look mum I can read this whole paragraph' then 'look mum I can read this whole page."

>43M: "We have started to read chapter books and he corrects me if I say a word wrong."

>58M: "One day he brought me his drawing and said 'look, I wrote my name on the other side'.

>7F: "On a shopping trip some months before her third birthday, [she] asked me "what's a BBQ?" I asked her what she meant. She pointed up to a notice in the supermarket and told me "That says, "It's time for a BBQ"…"

>24F: "I didn't know she could read until she picked up a Dr Seuss book and read it to me. Within weeks she was reading books to her 3-year-old sister."

>32F: "when I was finished with the series, she picked up the first one and started reading. I asked her how she knew what the words were and she said, 'I don't know, I just know them.'"

38F: "Suddenly she started to read books to us – board books that she'd had as a baby with simple language. I bought her some of the Ladybird *I Can Read By Myself* books ... she suddenly wanted to read to us a lot, and worked her way through the first three levels within a few weeks. Then she stopped wanting to read to us as abruptly as she started."

28Fam: "He recently read me a chapter of *Horrid Henry*."

22F: "The whole series (24 books plus specials) were on the shelf spines only showing, and she asked which one she needed. They all have numbers on the spine so I told her the last one we had read was number 7 from which she worked out she needed number 8 and went along the shelf looking for it. On finding it, she absent-mindedly said the title "Claw". She could only have known that by recognising the word as I didn't know what it was called. As far as I know she had no idea that was the name she was looking for either."

Observation

Sometimes parents observed behaviour that indicated that their child's relationship to written language had changed.

3M: "He wrote lots of phonetic messages and labels and it is possible to see in these how he was refining his understanding of the way letters and words work in English."

6M: "One day when he was sitting looking at a joke book, I realized he was reading it."

54M: "one afternoon (he was 8), I remember hearing him laughing away to himself. He was sitting on a chair in the living room. So I went and looked over his shoulder to see what he was doing. He was "reading" *Calvin and Hobbs*. And really reading. Many of the words were big words."

25F: "We noticed many, many months after trying Hooked on Phonics that she snuck the Hooked on Phonics books to her room. We pretended not to know she had them and didn't broach the subject. A few months later, she was voluntarily reading aloud."

Parents also noticed very subtle changes that indicated interest or changing reactions to the written word:

27F: "I always remember my daughter picking up very quickly on the big bright lights of the supermarket names."

22F: "During this time, though, we also noticed a shift in her choice of bedtime story book."

Questions

One particular way in which parents were able to observe their children's relationship with the written word was through the questions which they asked. It is possible to extrapolate quite a lot from the kind of questions that children ask – what they are thinking about, the terms in which they are thinking and also their reading aspirations; what it is that they may want to be able to read for themselves.

22F: "The change was really subtle – yes she started asking whether shops had their names on the front and other 'word' questions."

20F: "She often asks what words say when we are out and about."

57M: "He wanted to be able to read game cards, so he went asking for what was written, I knew he was able to read when he didn't come anymore."

8M: "He recognised words from about the age of 5 but showed no interest in reading until he was 10 when he suddenly stopped asking us to read his Beano as he wanted to do it for himself."

Children's own report

Sometimes children made their own assessment of what they could and could not do. This kind of self-assessment encompasses within it the child's own perception of what reading is and what it means to be a reader. This is a dimension to assessment that cannot exist very easily in external assessment made by another person. In this sense, self-assessment carries forward the theme of individuality that parents talked about. Children are not just individual in terms of when and why and how they learn to read, but are also individuals in terms of what it means to them personally to be 'a reader'.

> 10Fam: "At about the age of 3 we found her surrounded by books in their bedroom and announced "Mummy I can read" and so she could."
>
> 16M: "He stopped me half way through [the reading scheme] and announced he could read. I could hardly believe it but it was true."
>
> 25M: "As he was 6 years old, one Sunday morning he called 'Mama, I am at page 61!'"
>
> 50M: "My son tells me he IS learning to read and I will leave my trust in that!"
>
> 13F: "At 10 I saw her holding a book and I asked what it was. She said it was the book she'd read over the weekend. And that was that. She could read."

These types of assessment differ from the formal age-related, measuring of progressive skills that accompany the standard trajectory view of reading in a number of important ways.

Notably the kinds of informal assessments above always take place within a context of how that child sees reading, is using reading, is thinking about reading and feels about reading. This is a context which is missing from standardised assessment but it may be the most important thing about reading – the child's own relationship to the written word. How children view reading themselves lies much more to the forefront of both informal learning and informal assessment. Children's own aspirations, feelings, projections about their own accomplishments are able to form part of the assessment. In short the informal means of assessment tell us a lot more than a quantitative judgement about what level a child can read at in a test.

Informal assessment allows that a child's relationship with reading and with words is not a set one, but something that shifts in importance and emphasis and desirability as part of life rather than a set plan which must be accommodated, in a particular way, alongside life. This aspect of informal assessment confronts the idea of reading as a skill that exists independently of the people that use it.

Informal assessment is not invasive; it is not intimidating or pressurising. It does not threaten the principles of child paced, child led learning or of following the child's own interests and of emphasising the pleasure in reading. What this type of informal assessment is not able to do is to provide a standard base from which children can be compared with one another or with some pre-decided norm. It cannot act as a measure or a means of predication. Informal assessment is based on the here and now. It does not presuppose a given path that learning to read must take. It is not a measure of progress and cannot tell us what a child has already done or what he or she will do next. As such it is a big break away from assessment as currently understood and used in schools. Whether this is a good thing, and whether this kind of assessment can be considered adequate or appropriate brings us back to the question of why we want to assess children's learning in the first place. It also brings us back to the question of how we conceptualise learning itself, because in order for assessment to be meaningful at all these two things have to fit together. As such assessment itself is a secondary question which we can only address once we have formed a view on how learning takes place at home. In practical terms the home educating families in this research have found ways of assessing that accord with their views on learning to read.

Late reading

Perhaps the most dreaded educational assessments of all is so called 'late' reading. Learning to read late is the harbinger of big educational trouble. Children in school who are judged behind in reading face enormous difficulties. Those who are not reading at the expected level in primary school are subject to increasing levels of intervention which may be very stressful for the child concerned and the track record for which is not impressive. For children who arrive in secondary school still not meeting the appropriate age related target, the outlook is very bleak. Children in this situation rarely recover the lost ground and the consequences of poor reading spread across the curriculum (Slavin et al, 2009). Poor exam results and loss of confidence are serious detrimental factors carried forward into post-school life.

The designation of 'late' reading rests on the acceptance of the standard learning trajectory. From this representation, age related targets can be read off and if a child is behind the given point on the curve then 'late' reading can be diagnosed. The discussion and evidence above however, questions the accuracy of this depiction of learning. Whilst it may apply to some children it certainly does not represent many of the experiences of home educating families whose children go on to be successful and happy readers. If we are to re-think the utility of the standard learning trajectory we must simultaneously question the designation of 'late' reading. There were many children in this sample who learned to read over the age of seven (the designated school norm) and whose reading followed different but equally successful paths.

Whilst a child in school will receive five or six years of reading instruction before being expected to read a text with the language and vocabulary of say, a Harry Potter book, children at home might be reading such a text as their first reading or very shortly after beginning to read. At home a child who is not reading at 8, 9, 10, 11, 12 or older may become a proficient reader on par with age expected norms within months. These children would be counted as 'late' readers by school standards however simply applying this label does not describe or explain how very different their experiences can be from the standard expectations.

Learning to read at a later age deserves to be treated as a different experience, not the same experience at an older age and some parents noted this in comments about how 'later' readers can be quite different to younger readers:

> 22F: "I have learned that late readers become proficient very, very fast."
>
> 14F: "within a month [of beginning reading age 10] she was reading at grade level, within five years she was writing college papers and getting great marks on them."

It really cannot be stressed enough how different these experiences are to those of children in school. Re-thinking learning to read must take this important evidence into account; if we do not then we are doing an immense disservice to all the children whose lives are blighted both in school and beyond by reading difficulties. This important subject will be returned to in a later chapter.

The earlier, the better?

In main stream education the view taken of reading is nearly always that the sooner children begin to read the better. Certainly learning to read late is a problem to be avoided at all costs. Some of the families in the sample voiced the opposite opinion. These were parents who actually felt that it was better for children to learn later:

> 18M: "There are a lot of things that can be lost when you learn to read, like the ability to memorise, storytelling, and your own imagination so it should not be rushed."
>
> 30M: "Don't force reading on a child, it is a very special time to NOT be able to read as a child, when their world is not intruded on by advertisements and headlines etc. The child will soon make it clear when they want to

know more."

37Fam: "My second son is very eloquent on the difference learning to read made to him. He felt that reading somehow 'closed down' a part of his brain associated with imaginative play. He tried to retain his imaginative world for as long as possible and so finally read approaching adolescence – 12/13"

It is very easy amongst the educational talk of gains and achievements to think that more is always better and to see learning as the straight forward stock piling of knowledge. Elsewhere I have argued that learning implies losses as well as gains; we give up other possibilities in order to do or see things in a particular way (Pattison, 2016). According to this argument, learning to read is a closing down process as well as an opening up one and the parents above speak almost in protective terms of how they expect reading to impact on their children. This discussion will be continued in the next chapter through a consideration of the expectations and pressures that surround children's reading.

Chapter Eight

Expectations, pressure and child paced, child led philosophies of education

Social Pressure

The standard reading trajectory discussed in Chapter Six is more than an educational norm. It is a highly influential, extremely powerful cultural expectation and a potent political tool. Reading is deemed a key educational achievement, indeed perhaps **the** key achievement of primary education. More than this, reading is seen both nationally and internationally as a sign of cultural and individual advancement. Literacy levels have been linked with intelligence (Long, 2009), socio-economic potential, personal liberty (National Literacy Trust, 2012), social class (Long 2009); and on a national or social level with development, political engagement, economic growth, gender equality (UNESCO, 2006), and women's rights (Blunden, 2004). Early reading is often deemed a sign of intelligence, and is connected to the 'correct' kind of upbringing whilst late reading is seen as an indication of special educational needs and/or an inadequate home environment.

There is however, slightly more to reading expectations than the progressive curve that has come to stand for 'normal' development. Reading and writing are the tools of formal schooling. They are together the vehicles of transmission and practice, of testing and evaluation, the audit trail of work done, the proof that education has taken place. There is no *a priori* reason as to why education should be conducted almost exclusively through the medium of the written word but given that this is the case it is vital for the needs of schooling that children can read and write and can do so to the standard that the school requires for its own ends. The argument that schools teach children to read and write because these are skills they need in the wider world is the tip of an iceberg in which formal education itself has served to reify and reinforce, rather than simply react, to many of the links society makes between literacy and personal, social and economic success. As Harvey Graff has put it;

"Literacy is overvalued because of the very structure of formal schooling– schooling that, in Bruner's words, involves learning 'out of the context of action, by means that are primarily symbolic.' The currency of schools is words – words ... that are shaped up for the requirements of literacy."

(Graff, 1987, p18)

If a home educated child is not reading according to the 'normal' expectations this can be taken as a sign that their educational provision is lacking and that parents are not fulfilling their educational duties (Kunzman, 2009) and indeed there have now been calls for school style reading instruction to be a minimum criteria imposed on home education in the UK (Monk 2009). The desire to 'get children reading' is a full blown force. It is extremely difficult to ask people – parents, teachers, politicians, educational researchers, the general public to re-think reading. Its status is almost unassailable.

It is not simply children who are under pressure to become readers however. Modern western childhood is often characterized as an intensive project which will reflect the capacities of the parent as much as that of the child (Abboud and Kim, 2011). The extent to which the parents of schooled children are also regarded as educators may be open to question but there is in general an increasing emphasis on 'parenting' as a verb implying the active nature of what is expected of a (good) parent. As Judith Suissa has pointed out to simply be a parent is no longer regarded as adequate. She goes on to argue how "the role and nature of the parent–child relationship is conceived in western cultures today is largely the result of political and institutional changes regarding education" (Suissa, 2006, p66). The pressure of fulfilling social and political ideas about being a good parent is unlikely to be greater anywhere than in home education where parents are actively and voluntarily taking front-line responsibility for their child's education as well as other aspects of their well-being.

Given all this, it is small wonder that in the atmosphere of excitement, discovery and interest that filled the questionnaire returns there were also comments that revealed the stress and pressure parents frequently felt themselves under as they swam against the tide of common opinion on learning to read. This pressure could come from the wider family or from outside the family but also from parents themselves as they chewed over their educational choices.

> 56F: "As her parent, getting flak from other family members and seeing her schooled contemporaries starting to read, the last few months since she turned 5 have been a bit difficult. I keep having to stop myself from pushing reading instruction on her – no matter what my philosophy or stubborn desire not to allow the rest of the world to dictate how I raise my children, the mores of society do encroach and make me doubt myself!"

The feeling that children should be at least beginning to read aged five or six can be overwhelming and for parents, worry and anxiety, could translate into action intended to fulfil that norm:

> 78M: "I put a huge amount of pressure on my son when he was 5 and 6 to learn to read"

> 29Fam: "A. read later than her big sister so I started to worry and sit down and try to 'do phonics' with her."

> 36Fam: "I also attempted to force her to learn how to put the letters together to form words instead of just reading and answering her questions because I did not know better."

> 57F: "When she was five I began to panic because she still couldn't read and I forced reading lessons on her that she wasn't ready for."

Some parents offered practical coping strategies – don't listen to the criticisms, don't compare to others or to educational standards - and relax:

> 49M: "Go at their pace, don't make comparisons with other children."
>
> 62F: "Being really relaxed about her being able to read and being ready for it to take a long time with no pressure also had a big impact I believe."
>
> 2Fam: "Not listening to my mother-in-law's concerns was another good idea."
>
> 6Fam: "It is so lovely to just love your kids and sit back and watch them unfold at just the perfect time for them. I wish I could have had this same freedom."
>
> 44Fam: "We have seen it happen years later in other children who had the good fortune to have parents who did not push them or freak out (much) when their children weren't reading at 7 or 9 or whatever."
>
> 30F: "[I learned] to leave her be and not worry. I know that she can do it when she wants to."

Others pointed out that parents were not the only ones under pressure; assumptions about reading filter through to children too, potentially putting them under stress as well. Some parents felt that an important part of their role was to protect children from these ideas:

> 6Fam: "They need a lot of support in a culture that is so focused on early reading and protection from criticism especially from fearful relatives etc."

Despite the pressurized climate and the expectations surrounding reading however, home educators have re-thought reading and their convictions about other learning possibilities gave many the strength needed to be different. The thinking from these families constitutes an approach characterised by the bringing together of three principles: the acceptance of individuality, child paced and child led learning. This is not to say that all families who responded actively expressed adherence to these ideals but they were so frequently articulated that they formed an overarching message.

All children are different

Children in school do not have a choice about reading instruction. Nor for that matter do schools or teachers. The teaching and testing of reading are laid out in the national curriculum from the earliest phases of formal education. Curriculum planning is a complicated business in which the needs of institutions, political bodies, wider communities, the educational buzz criteria of objectives, achievements and outcomes all have to be accommodated. Despite the mantra of individualized education, the shadowy figure of the 'learner' who inhabits the rhetoric of the curriculum is inevitably a standardized, normalised child whose learning must answer to the needs of others.

At home things are very different. At home parents have to make their own active decisions about when, how and whether to implement reading instruction. Judith Suissa has argued the difference between the generalized advice that parents receive about various aspects of child rearing with the first person position of being the particular person, me, who is in a relationship with a particular child, my child. Parents she argues must make a "creative response" (Suissa, 2006, p75) to a person they know; not follow general rules about a hypothetical, stylized child. In institutionalized education individuality can be paid only lip service; at home it is very often the value that drives decision making. And hand in hand with the acceptance of individuality must go the recognition of difference.

Thirty-two parents, including several who had had diverse experiences between children in their own family, stressed that learning to read is an individual matter in which acknowledging difference is a bedrock principle:

> 34Fam: "Be aware of individual differences."

43Fam: "Reading happens differently for different people."

1Fam: "It is very different for different children."

22M: "I think it is different with every person of course."

44M: "It's different for everyone just as learning to walk, or talk is different for everyone."

80M: "Each child is very different in how they learn to read and when they are ready."

74M: "I also think it is important to acknowledge the difference in children."

The importance of this difference was sustained whether or not children were actively taught. Parents who opted to actively teach often talked about how different approaches and methods suited different children:

2F: "you can adapt the method to suit the individual child".

12M: "No one system works for all"

1Fam: "Every child learns differently. Some children need phonics to learn and some don't"

5M: "There are many and varied approaches to reading, and if one thing doesn't work, try another"

21M: "I've seen children come to reading at many different ages ... being responsive to a child's individual learning strengths is a good place to start."

The sum of these parents' argument is that there can be no one right, best or pre-determined way to learn to read:

16Fam: "I find it amazing that someone can learn in a totally different way to someone else and my experience of home education shows me very clearly that one size does not fit all."

27F: "All kids are different and learn according to their own personal time frame and they all learn using different styles and approaches."

> 80M: "Each child is very different in how they learn to read and when they are ready."

So, recognising individuality leads to the acceptance of difference between children and this in turn entails that there can be no objective 'best' way to learn to read or any optimum standardised time at which to do so. The logic of this line of thought leads inevitably to either an implicit or explicit argument against the standardised learning trajectory and against the adoption of mass implemented learning programmes:

> 8Fam: "School based pedagogy is not the only way."

> 7F: "I am frankly horrified by the 'one-size-fits-all' initiative-driven approaches that teachers are often forced to adopt – and subsequently discard to make way for the next fad."

> 26F: "Children are ready for different skills at different ages and respecting that is vitally important to fostering a love of learning anything, including reading."

> 31Fam: "Learning to read is a very personal adventure and each person comes to it differently at different times and for different reasons and in different ways."

Child paced, child led learning

Instead, parents turned towards individualized learning expressed through philosophies and practices of child paced and child led learning.

Child paced

The children in this research learned to read between the ages of 18 months and 16 years. This is an extraordinarily wide window of learning compared to the rigidity of expectation experienced in school and, in itself, offers a radically different approach to reading. Across the spectrum of teaching to untaught there was nothing laissez-faire about child paced learning; rather it was a thought out philosophy:

> 31F: "I honestly believe that all children benefit from being

> allowed to dictate their own pace."
>
> 64M: "It is much better to let your child set the pace."
>
> 10F: "People really do come to it in their own time."

In discussing child paced learning many parents evoked the idea of readiness. Theories of reading readiness were proposed in the 1950s and 60s and involved teachers instructing in skills that were thought to underlie successful reading such as various motor skills and auditory and visual discrimination (Morrow 2012). However, the way in which parents used the term 'readiness' was quite different. Parents used the idea of readiness very broadly to refer to physical and mental and/or emotional states as well as to attributes like motivation.

Some parents talked about readiness in terms of a state of mental maturation:

> 13Fam: "When their brain is ready it's a smooth process. It just takes patience."
>
> 32Fam: "We can teach them all we want, but like so many skills and milestones they will achieve it when they are developmentally ready."

Others saw readiness to be emotional rather than embodied:

> 25F "emotional readiness to read is more important than his or her intellectual readiness."

Others contrasted an intellectual readiness to a motivational state:

> 22F "wanting to learn to read is more important than 'being ready'."
>
> 23Fam: "When children are ready they will learn out of natural curiosity and not liking to be left out of this special thing that everyone else is enjoying."

Readiness was clearly a very important idea yet it was used in so many different ways that an identifiable definition did not emerge from the data. Instead it seems to be a term that parents use in an individual sense to describe the subjective 'rightness' of the time rather than an objective state of the child.

Many parents talked about the qualitative difference in experience between children who learned to read on a schedule and children who learned according to individual 'readiness', voicing the view that the former could bring about short term learning problems and/or longer term negative attitudes towards reading:

> 3Fam: "Children who are forced to read before they are ready may develop an aversion to reading"
>
> 74M: "Children will read when they are ready and pushing earlier can create unnecessary anxiety and reading stumbling blocks."
>
> 37M: "Pressing the 'need' to learn before the desire on the part of the child exists is futile and frustrating (which can potentially delay/eradicate the child's desire to learn and take away the joy of reading.)"
>
> 34F: "I think we force kids to read too early and make them anxious about themselves if they can't meet our schedule."
>
> 34M: "Forcing someone to read can do lasting damage. If a child is allowed to learn at their own pace with no pressure, not only will they learn to read but they will enjoy it too."
>
> 17M: "Fear (as in school children who are failing to learn) blocks learning."

By contrast, parents re-iterated their conviction that child paced learning was not only a nice, child-friendly approach but was also an educationally sound one providing, over the long term, a qualitatively superior education. This was because parents saw the pressure of keeping up with educational norms as an undermining of the enjoyment and love of reading which they hoped to nurture and which they ultimately saw as constituting successful reading:

> 45Fam: "It should be something they love to do, at their own pace; not something compulsory at a certain age."
>
> 5M: "Allow them to learn at their own pace, it turns them into people who love to read ... not people who suffer through it for points or a grade."
>
> 32F: "If the process is forced and /or the adult (parent or teacher) is anxious about the child's learning, the desire is usually removed from the equation. In those cases, reading becomes a task that has to be done to please someone else. The joy is gone."

Child led learning

In general, the question of child-led learning appeared to raise far fewer issues than did the matter of child-paced learning. Clearly parents felt pressure about the age at which their child learned to read far more strongly than they felt under duress to provide a certain kind of teaching or a certain kind of approach. The social and educational emphasis falls tellingly on the adherence to age related norms rather than on the kind of experience children have whilst learning.

Nearly all the parents expressed their interest in child-led learning and this was felt across the whole spectrum of approaches:

> 39F: "Back off and let the child lead."
>
> 68M: "I think a child-led approach is very important."
>
> 38F: "Letting her do it in her own time and in her own way."

Child-led learning covered everything from children asking to be taught, to showing a preference to a particular method, to rejecting teaching altogether, to devising their own approaches to reading.

For some the child's own self involvement in the process led to a qualitative distinction in what it means to learn to read:

> 15M:" When reading is taught it is not usually a self-discovery

and then is less likely to be embraced."

34F: "I believe a child needs to do it on their own."

Waiting for the child to lead the way meant that children's own curiosity, motivation and other emotions (such as impatience!) could all assist the learning process:

> 39Fam: "[she] got fed up of not being able to read and being bored waiting for me. She was a very impatient child!"
>
> 19F: "She is very nosy and always wanted to know what this sign said, what that poster said, what does that text message say, what does that email say and so on."
>
> 31M: "He is motivated by a desire to read words on things that interest him."
>
> 10Fam: "When there was information they really wanted to get, that motivated them to learn."
>
> 8Fam: "Feeling the need inside themselves for either information or curiosity/enjoyment."

Extending the argument further still, some parents linked their child-paced/child-led philosophy to a theory of natural learning. They argued that as learning is a natural process and as reading is such an ongoing, ever present element in our culture, children would learn to read as a naturally occurring process:

> 10F: "She saw us reading all the time, we read to her a lot, we helped when asked and gave her unpressured time to come to it. You couldn't stop them from reading, given all that!"
>
> 58M: "It comes naturally. You can't help but pick it up. It's all around.
>
> 9Fam: "Reading is a fundamental skill that will be acquired in a world where the written word is all around them."
>
> 18M: "It is very difficult to not learn to read in our society."
>
> 28M: "I believe that in this information rich age every child WILL learn to read in their own way and at their own

pace, regardless of methods used or actual 'teaching'."

35M: "It is part of what seems to be an internal motivation to master the world around them and because our culture uses the written word, it just happens."

In this view learning will unfold naturally and intervening in the process would constitute a disturbance that would ultimately interfere with, rather than assist, the process.

44Fam: "It is a natural one [process] when supported and not thwarted."

36Fam: "Forcing a child to "learn" to read is counterproductive and interferes with their natural process."

30M: "Reading schemes get in the way of the child's own natural ways of progressing in their reading."

The nuances of teaching and not teaching, structure and autonomy have been discussed in Chapter Three. Many of the decisions which parents made about teaching or not teaching were based on, or tempered by, their interests in child led and child paced learning. It is through their adherence to these ideas that much of the challenge is made to both the standardised learning trajectory on which the age related norms of reading are based and to the idea that reading can be pursued through a best practice programme. The range of ensuing experience is able in turn to provide the basis from which the notion of reading as an objectively definable concept can be philosophically challenged.

Challenging the role of reading and writing in education

The medium of formal education is the written word. As stated at the beginning of this chapter it is very important for schools that children learn to read and write quickly and to the standard which school requires of them for its own ends. In other approaches to education the links between literacy and education are not nearly so necessary; there are other pedagogical tools including the verbal, the visual and the hands on as has been expressed in previous research (Thomas and Pattison 2007).

To argue that a child's education can be furthered without the need for a minimum standard of literacy is a view hard to maintain in the main stream. Contrary to this however, there were strong examples here of parents who clearly considered that their child not reading constituted no impediment to the progression of their education:

> 43Fam: "I do not think they have been disadvantaged by not being able to read, because I have been there to facilitate their interaction with life and learning and to assist them by reading information for them as necessary."
>
> 56M: "learning things at home does not rely entirely on reading."

As already discussed in Chapter Five most children were read to, many prolifically. On the whole parents considered this to be a major contribution to their children's education. Certainly there is no reason as to why the information and knowledge picked up by children through being read to should not be equal to, or even greater, than that which they would have acquired by reading for themselves. Parents also emphasised how much they talked to their children and interacted with them; an interaction which they commonly saw as educational albeit embedded in personal relationships and everyday life. The emphasis on conversation and discussion highlighted both the possibilities of education at home and were telling of the context of home education in which long stretches of time are available for such conversations; an opportunity not generally a feature of school life.

Other ways in which education can be furthered without literacy - in the pursuit of diverse and myriad hobbies, activities, sports, games, imaginative play, crafts, watching TV, visiting museums and places of interest and more have been discussed in previous work (Thomas and Pattison 2007) and many are also touched on in preceding chapters. It is possible that without the emphasis on reading and writing children's education actually becomes more wide ranging – able to foster other means of learning, enquiry, consideration and investigation which have strengths and possibilities not exploited through literacy. Forms of education based on experiential learning or techniques such as Socratic dialogue spring to mind, amongst others, and are deserving of a fuller exploration in the context of home education. In addition, we need to take account of the possibilities which new forms of technology are opening up in their ability to transcend and transform reading and writing processes. Suffice to end the discussion here by re-affirming the considerable educational means which are available aside from the written word.

Chapter Nine

Brothers and sisters and what happens in families

The previous chapter discussed how important parents felt the recognition of difference between children to be and how this, in itself, led to challenges to main stream thinking. In this chapter that theme is taken a little further by looking at the difference between children in the same family and exploring ideas around the nature of this difference.

A number of parents commented on the differences they had noted between siblings both in the ways in which they learned to read and the ages at which they learned to read:

> 16F: "They all learn differently ... I have two 7-year-old sons who are also on the reading journey and they are both doing it completely differently from their sister and each other!"
>
> 31Fam: "At age 6, I tried to use the same method as the first son was taught in school, figuring that what had worked for one would work for the other, but that turned out not to be true."
>
> 43Fam: "I have one child who learnt very phonetically by spelling words out and breaking them down into their sounds, and one who learnt by recognising whole words."
>
> 26M: "[one son] hates phonics, but [his brother] quite likes it."
>
> 14Fam: "Each child was different, one broke the words into letters and puzzled them out, and the other learned whole words."

Differences in children's attitudes and approaches to reading were marked but with the powerful presence of age related norms never very far away, it was the difference in ages within the same family which are perhaps the most striking. The ages at which siblings learned to read could vary tremendously within families; the most extreme example in the data being that of a family of four children who learned to read aged 4, 7, 11 and 12. Between the youngest and the oldest reader lies a gap of 8 years. As discussed in the previous chapter this could be quite nerve racking for parents but also raises the question of why this should be the case.

Explaining difference

Difference is generally understood as meaning difference between a child's reading and age related norms; thus children may be ahead or behind age expectations meaning that accounts of difference are seeking reasons for either a shortfall in, or an excess of, ability. Concentrating on the former, explanations for shortfalls in expectations of children's reading have generally fallen into two camps being usually attributed to either a deficit in the child or a deficit in their home environment.

Deficits within the child

Current mainstream understandings of reading contend that writing is speech transferred into the physical form of written letters which must then be decoded back to its original spoken form. This view underlies both phonic and whole word approaches to reading, although the latter has a vastly reduced following and is not used in state run schools in the UK. Under phonics methods children must learn to associate different letter combinations with the different sounds which make up speech. Differences or difficulties in reading are attributed to the ease with which children learn to make the letter sound association and this has led to the thesis that the ability to hear individual sounds in speech (phenomes) is crucial. As one leading reading expert puts it, "awareness of the phonological structure of one's spoken language is clearly fundamental to the acquisition of literacy" (Goswami, 2009, p138). From here she is able to pinpoint the source of reading differences, "developmental studies of reading acquisition across languages show that individual differences in reading development are (for the most part) governed by individual differences in phonological skills" (Goswami, 2009, p 135). So the ability to read rests with the capacity of the child to distinguish between sounds and then to recognise these sounds as they are represented by a written letter or group of letters.

Despite its main stream dominance, there are difficulties with this point of view. Gerald Coles for example has written a blistering critique of the evidence based studies that link phonological awareness with reading prowess arguing that correlation has been taken as causation; children who are good readers are able to break down words phonetically but this does not mean that their ability to do so precedes or enables their ability to read. Furthermore, Coles contends, there is no long term difference in reading ability between children trained in these skills and children not trained in them (Coles, 2000). Some parents in the study also questioned the supposed link between 'sub-skills' and the general ability of reading, doubts expressed in Chapter Three:

> 70: "you can pass tests fairly well without actually having learned what you were supposed to learn."

In other words, children may be able to show phonics skills but this may not enhance their reading ability as this parent found:

> 29F: "She knew all the letter sounds but couldn't blend them together."

However, phonics has been accepted by main stream education as the route to successful reading and the importance of phonological awareness as the cause of reading differences along with it. If a child is unable to demonstrate phonological awareness, then he or she is said to have reading difficulties or to be at risk of them. Of course this argument only holds where phonics is the sole means of understanding what reading is and equally is the only method through which reading is approached. As discussed in Chapter Three, in this research families approached reading from many educational and philosophical standpoints. Although phonics approaches are well represented they are not exclusive; many parents disagreed with phonics and others were flexible in their thinking about phonics. Where children were explicitly taught by their parents mixed methods or methods not involving phonics were frequently used.

In families where no method of learning to read was invoked children may have developed their own phonetic theories such as this boy:

> 6M: "He learned the letter names by himself and then noticed the letter sounds."

However, if phonemic awareness does not come easily to them, children are unlikely to spontaneously follow a phonetic route into reading. Many children in this research do not seem to have learned to read via phonics methods. Given this, differences in levels of phonemic awareness offer, at best, an incomplete picture of the differences between siblings noted here.

Deficits within the environment

It is widely accepted in current thinking on learning to read that the provision of a literate environment is essential. This kind of socio-cultural argument has led to research on children's home lives including such factors as how many books children own, how much other members of the family read, whether or not children are taken to the library, whether parents read in front of their children and a whole host of other issues which are said to produce a conducive environment which will introduce children to reading and set them on the approved path of literacy learning. Such is the strength of this idea in current thinking that it is now believed that "the strongest predictor of children's early literacy development is provision for children's literacy development at home" (Browne, 2009, p229 – 230).

This kind of thinking distils down to parents in the form of advice about how to behave with their children in order to help schools achieve their literacy goals. A BBC website for instance tells parents "reading with your child is vital. Research shows that it's the single most important thing you can do to help your child's education" (BBC, 2012). The purpose behind reading aloud is explicitly given that children will do better in school as a result (*Children Better Prepared For School If Their Parents Read Aloud To Them*, 2008). Advice given to parents from schools can be surprisingly specific including guidance on how to listen to their child read (Browne, 2009). The central argument is that children are critically affected by their environment and by the interactions which take place within that environment. The message is very simple. Perhaps too much so.

Parents who wrote about more than one child pointed out that siblings did not necessarily react in the same way to the same environment:

> 23M: "It varies for each child. My younger son, now 4, has had the same environment as his brother but has not just 'picked up' reading."
>
> 45Fam: "Having one child who learnt at 3 and another who learnt at 7, I've come to realise that you can't fit children into preconceived moulds of learning behaviour; it depends on the individual abilities and wishes of each child."

The difficulty with the socio-cultural arguments (at least in the terms in which they are presented to parents) is that they assume a one-way effect between the environment and children in that environment. What is missing is the effect which children themselves have on their environment. There are many examples from the questionnaires in which children expressed likes and dislikes about the role of literacy in their lives and parents changed their behaviour or altered their ideas in accordance with this. The following examples show how children resist or reshape their environments and/or the interaction offered by parents:

> 23Fam: "He has never let me read to him, and still does not want me to"
>
> 21M: "When he was 18 months he would sit in my lap and ask me to write letters for him."
>
> 58M: "My son had no interest in learning his letters or writing

though he LOVES books."

43M: "We have to fight to turn the lights off at night often as late as 11pm as he wants to read…he reads through meals, in queues, wherever we are."

1Fam: "Chooses not to read much at all. Says he would rather do other things."

As discussed in Chapter Four some children rejected their parents offers to teach them, others did not want to be read to. Most children chose their own reading material and the extent to which they wished to engage with it. They sought out particular kinds of experiences and eschewed others. The following description details how one boy carved out his own literary environment from the things that appealed to him as well as the opportunities on offer:

7Fam: "He spends many hours alone in his room listening to Harry [Potter] on CD or to anything he can get his hands on … he roams from person to person begging us to read … He has opinions on all of the books … he tells us stories. He draws detailed pictures that take hours to complete as he tells the story that creates the picture. He has fully-formed characters already in his mind that just pop out."

Such examples show how children are active agents, responding to, but also shaping, influencing, changing and creating their own environment.

Throughout the data parents continuously pointed out the individuality of children who bring to reading their own motivation, purposes, needs, wishes and interests, carrying through the argument that every child is different regardless of what kind of environment they occupy or with whom they share that environment:

9F: "I have two children, one who began to read fluently at 6 the other who at 12 is beginning to move towards fluency. That has been more informative than almost any

> other thing about learning. My elder child has not lived in a different environment to my younger child, but clearly has had a different response to that environment. Having such a natural experiment (with an n of 2) has demonstrated that the expectations that all children should read by age x are faulty."

People are not produced by a social environment, instead their interactions with that environment are complicated and on-going, dependant on numerous factors including each individuals unique placing in terms of time, culture, experience and his or her own capacities for response (Olssen, 2008). It is an argument neatly summarised in terms of reading by the following parent:

> 22F: "How they see the world, how they think, what they deem important at any particular time, their personality, their stages of development etc, etc all have a distinct bearing on how the written word impacts on their consciousness and a change in any of these things alters their relationship with words, not just as a whole but at any moment in time."

This parent's words clearly indicate the nuanced understanding of reading allowed by one of the central themes arising from this research: that is the foregrounding of the principle that all children should be seen as distinct individuals who are distinguished by the differences between them rather than by their commonality. The evidence from families gives even stronger grounds to challenge the homogeneity of experience which is postulated by standardised approaches and by the standardised trajectory of learning to read. When it comes to considering siblings, variations within families are no different to variations between families. Every child is an individual. Differences do not need to be problematized as they are inevitable and therefore normal.

Chapter Ten

Coming out of school and special educational needs

A number of children in the research had previously spent some time in school and for some of these children, reading had been a factor in the decision to begin home educating, although the problems encountered and their consequences, were varied.

For some the difficulties were to do with the approaches to reading and programmes presented in school:

> 16 F: "The reading instruction in school was more detrimental than helpful ... just about every reading program that was tried at school was a failure for my older daughter... many of the programs I saw used in school were actually turning kids off reading."
>
> 50F: "I had no choice but to send her to school and I watched a torturous process in trying to force her to read, knowing it was not the best way."
>
> 28M: "After three weeks of attending school where they used the phonics method he decided it was too slow and boring... phonics totally confused him and slowed his reading down as he would stop at every letter and sound it out and got very confused when he realised that hardly any English words are spelled 'fon-et-ic-lee'".

Part of the issue, as the above quotes illustrate, and as discussed previously, is that reading in school (at least in the UK) largely consists of phonics. This is not to say that schools and teachers do not recognise the number of different strategies which can be brought to bear on reading; the 2004 HMI report on reading in primary schools explicitly recognised the importance of introducing other strategies alongside phonics (Browne, 2009). Nevertheless, phonics forms the backbone of school instruction and if a child does not 'get' phonics there is no replacement for it. Other strategies such as playing games and listening to stories are supplementary; they do not stand in its stead. Children who are not progressing well with phonics are likely to receive more and more of the same kind of instruction in the same method. Some parents felt that this resulted in a legacy of difficulties:

> 13M: "Our daughter was taught to read but on entering Primary School the insistence on Jolly Phonics techniques left us with problems of reading and writing which is still an on-going problem"

Other children seem to have lost momentum or motivation whilst in school:

> 16Fam: "It was sad to see the motivation disappear when forced to read 'age appropriate' material at school and to be held back in his reading because he was going too far ahead."

> 43M: "He started to use 'easy' readers at school but wasn't thrilled and often would refuse to read. He was given 'key words' to learn and hated them".

> 12M: "[He] learned to read while at home. Very basic – three, four letter words, three – four word sentences at age 3 – 4. Entered public school at head start level … and deemed very well prepared for Kindergarten already [but] by Kindergarten losing interest; by 2nd grade below grade level".

> 47F: "There is something about school which switches off motivation".

For other children experiences in school had an emotional impact which undermined their self-confidence and created stress and anxiety:

> 54M: "He loved Jr Kindergarten and Kindergarten but really started to baulk when he was required to "sit still and learn" in Gr. 1 (age 6). He also was struggling with spelling, he could read the words and knew them well when we went over them at home, but when it came time to do the spelling test (they did one each week –

ugh!) he would consistently come home with three or four out of 10. I could see him already beginning to feel like a failure. So when we moved out of the school district in May of his Grade 1 year … we simply did not put him back in the school system."

34F: "The school thought she couldn't read at all and had her thinking she was stupid and had me very worried. They were trying to get her to read books meant for 5 year olds. One day I handed her a book aimed at her age (7 at the time) and she just read it. She surprised even herself."

21M: "His English teacher at secondary school tried to force him every lesson to read in front of the class, enough to put him off reading altogether, caused a lot of intolerable stress for him, never mind the humiliation and embarrassment. He is happy now but we are trying to reverse years of failure at school."

41F: "[she] left school due to the teachers that kept saying she couldn't do anything right … They told her to stand up in class and the teacher went 'you can't read. You get a zero.'"

In some cases parents felt that not only was the school not helping but was actually holding their child back or had even caused him or her to regress:

16Fam: "He started with the Oxford reading scheme and was progressing with those books. We then moved to another school and despite my protests they restarted the scheme from the beginning and my son rebelled against this as far as he was concerned he'd already done it. This was taken as he needed extra help … when my son came out of school 15 months later he could not read at all."

45 F: "The school in the Netherlands forced her to read at a lower level than she wanted (she was termed a 'slow

reader') and it nearly took away her pleasure in reading. We objected and told her that at home she could read at whatever speed she wanted".

44F "Unfortunately when she began school, her teacher did not seem to believe that she could read, and made her look at picture books until the second term when she gave her a list of high frequency words to learn at home – all of which she had already learned."

45M: "He went to school for one term and regressed... A noisy class room with lots of distractions is not the right place for many!"

Some parents felt that school created rather than solved reading problems by expecting children to learn in a particular way and/or at a particular time. The existence of these expectations means that difficulties are created when they are not met and these 'difficulties' then need to be 'solved'. Without the particular expectations, there would never have been a problem to rectify. This mother wrote about her daughter who started reading at home when she was ten:

13F: "I think she was probably suffering from some kind of childhood dyslexia and that if she had been at school she would have been singled out as a child with reading problems. By doing nothing it all seems to have sorted itself out."

Some parents felt that it is school itself which sets up reading problems; not just in the handling of individual children but in its inherent approaches and structure:

78M: "they are made to read too early in school, this quashes their enthusiasm ... I am a teacher so using that experience too."

54M: "I have learned that school does not meet the needs of every child in their best interests."

71M: "I really think he has learned despite me and certainly despite the dreaded school schemes ... [he] hates school reading schemes!"

45M: "I feel schools make reading hard. Kids don't want to be force-fed. If you want a kid to dislike anything, teach it to them while they're chained inside to a desk on a beautifully warm sunny day in the spring."

26F: "She hated reading the school text books and wanted to read what she wanted to read about ... the things that they read should interest them not just the teacher."

42M: "I think that schools try to teach many children to read before they are ready to learn. This leads to frustration and school is no longer a place of learning."

Special educational needs

Where children experience difficulties learning to read in school, special educational needs are often diagnosed as being the cause of those difficulties. Parents who talked about the influence of special educational needs on their decision to take children out of school fell into two camps: those who felt their child had been unjustifiably or unhelpfully labelled with special educational needs and those who felt that their child's special needs had not been adequately recognised or addressed within the system.

The following parents felt the special educational needs which had been diagnosed in their children had been incorrect or unhelpful:

51M: "initially at school, misdiagnosed as globally impaired, (delayed language skills) ... he has had numerous labels from delayed language skills, SLI [specific language impairment] globally impaired (he was never globally impaired) independent psychology report – dyslexia, S&L [speech and language] report, severe S&L impairment... I have now told them to send the labels back to their owners"

44M: "the principal called me in her office and informed me that he would not be allowed to return to school until he was being medicated for supposed behaviour problems. He has been educated at home ever since and is doing well – working at or above grade level in almost all subjects."

77M: "Educated at school but since he started teachers labelled him how they wanted, any information or support I tried to give they didn't take even half of it in."

60M: "Home educated since the age of 9. He attended a French language school from age 4 to 8 but his language difficulties became apparent during the last year. He was also identified as ADD. We tried moving him to an English Language program for 3 months but he became totally frustrated. The school seemed to be writing off his ability to learn to read so we began to homeschool."

16Fam: "I probably should point out here that my son is physically disabled and the second school seemed to automatically assume that this meant my son wasn't able to do what he was asked."

Some parents questioned how, what they saw as a natural variation, became the subject of difficulties, disorders and labelling in school:

66F [I have learned] "That 'learning disabled' and dyslexia' are way over used by the public school system ... I have children who read well by age 6 and children who did not learn to read until they were in their teens" ... (family of 8)

54F: "Interestingly despite the fact that I went to school I did not start reading until I too was 8 and reading took off like a rocket for me in the same way as it happened for my daughter. Yet I was labelled as 'educationally subnormal' during primary school." (Mother of daughter who began to read aged 8)

Other parents felt that school could be insensitive to children's (special) needs. This could be through the imposition of a uniform learning schedule which sets expectations which their child could not meet:

> 70M: "[at] 11 [he] was diagnosed as dyslexic and suffering from school anxiety because of constant experiences of failure. He couldn't read second grade detective story or Mickey Mouse comic then despite shallow German orthography (we come from Germany)."

> 40Fam: "I have found that the creative/spatial/technical child (often a boy) learns to read at a later age. In school he/she may be labelled 'dyslexic'." (Mother of three children who learned to read aged between 10 and 12)

The pressurised atmosphere under which children were expected to reach reading norms was seen by some to compound the cycle of failure and special needs designations:

> 19M: "If given support and the freedom to read as much as they want in a pressure-free environment, children become readers, even if they have been diagnosed with a reading 'disability'"

> 29M: "If people outside of the child try to rush the process, it only ends with the child feeling frustrated and like a failure. Which does nothing more than set the child up to hate reading."

> 17M: "Fear (as in school children who are failing to learn) blocks learning."

> 74M: "Children will read when they are ready and pushing earlier can create unnecessary anxiety and reading stumbling blocks."

Some parents felt that schools are not able or willing to vary their approaches to reading in order to assist SEN children. This mother of three children whom she describes as dyslexic wrote:

> 3F: "The emphasis on early literacy considered necessary in schools, in spite of the availability of alternative technology that would make this unnecessary is

immensely damaging to children who are just as bright as their peers if not more so but are differently wired."

Another frustrated parent recounted how the handling of her son's SEN had led to far reaching labels but not the changes to teaching which she had hoped for:

51M: "I now realise that education psychologists do not recommend appropriate teaching methods and how powerful labels are."

Special educational needs are an emotive issue amongst home educators as well as for parents of children in school. However, there is a freedom amongst home educating families to address their children's reading 'difficulties' in more open ways than are generally available in schools. SEN, as Claire Penketh reminds us, are part of the educational thinking embedded in the schooling system. Their meaning and even existence away from this system is an open question:

"We need to continue to remind educators, at all levels, that people do not 'have' special educational needs. People may experience impairment but their educational needs are made special as a result of the ways in which we conceptualise and organise our education systems. The term 'Special Educational Needs' (SEN) refers to a set of systems for organising educational processes and allocating resources (Terzi 2010)."

(Penketh, 2014, p1486)

Away from this system, for example in the informal environment of the home, it is perfectly possible to organise educational resources and expectations in different ways and this was the reaction of many families who encountered what would in school be designated as special educational needs. The argument mirrors the challenges made to viewing reading as a method discussed in Chapter Three. Where method and expectation are conceived of in terms of variability rather than normalism the idea of 'reading problems' undergoes a transformation. Problems are created when children do not react to learning expectations in the predicted ways; for instance, if they do not catch on to the ideas of phonics or are not interested in engaging with them. Addressing the created problems is one way of approaching this situation but another is to couch expectations differently. As this parent put it:

> 8Fam: "Time usually solves most things: child not reading? Wait 6 months; still not reading? Wait 6 months, etc."

De-schooling

De-schooling is a term coined by Ivan Illich (1971) to describe the shift to non-institutionalised learning which he advocated. It is now often used by home educators to describe the period of change and adjustment when a child gives up formal schooling to begin home educating in a less structured or expectation driven way. Some parents found that children were insistent on this break; wanting nothing to do with reading whatsoever if their withdrawal from school had been triggered by reading issues:

> 16Fam: "I think the issues he had at school with reading did a lot of damage to his enjoyment of books. He loved to sit and listen to stories and now won't do that."

> 66M: "He loved having stories read to him until he went to school, then he began to hate reading."

Some children re-gained their interest in reading quite quickly, as was the case with the quote above where happily the mother reported:

> 66M "Now he has gained a lot of interest back."

Others felt that there were longer term consequences for things that had gone wrong in school:

> 16Fam: "I feel that because he was being forced to learn in a way that wasn't suitable for him he is now nearly ten and still is not a fluent reader"

Picking up reading again after difficulties in school often entailed a reversal of the situations that had led to those difficulties; for example, re-building confidence, allowing children to read what they wanted in their own time and in their own ways, seeking out enjoyment rather than achievement. Children also had the freedom to follow up their own ideas about reading and to establish or re-establish their own literacy interests:

> 5 M: "He knows now that he can do it at his own pace, he no longer feels stupid as he did when he was at school. The importance of confidence building was the main thing I learned."
>
> 10M: "Once he was out of school he appeared to learn quickly/improve quickly. However, since coming out of school we have realised he learnt by whole word memory rather than any phonic sound blend. Words out of context were unknown to him"
>
> 71M: "His reading has come on a lot more since he was at home and I feel this has been due to focus on books and stories rather than sounds."

In the questionnaire responses three stories stood out as documenting children who had had particularly difficult experiences in school. The following history is of a boy who was aged 11 at the time of the questionnaire:

> 34M: "He could not read and was behind in all areas, he became hyperactive, had concentration difficulties, stopped eating, developed behaviour problems, OCD, severe headaches etc. Was completely fine in school holidays and very distressed when returning to school. Began [home educating] second week of September and mental state and behaviour back to normal very quickly but instantly became hysterical if I tried to teach him to read. Continued to enjoy having stories read to him (I have always read books to my children on a daily basis) but was totally opposed to learning to read himself. ... In the end I decided to not try and get him to read at all. I continued to read to him and if he needed to write something I would let him dictate to me and I wrote it for him. We produced some excellent work this way.

> Whenever he wanted to know what something said I'd tell him and eventually I noticed that he was beginning to work things out for himself. He'd read signs, packets, text on his computer games and he liked to read the Ladybird Read-it-Yourself story books that only had very simple sentences in them (I think it was more from memory than actual reading but it gave him confidence). Then one day something clicked and he sat down by himself and read 'The Twits' from cover to cover. He's now able to read most things but does not enjoy reading in the way that my other son does, which I'm very saddened about."

Finally, this parent reflected that pressure on children to perform in school could have long-term detrimental consequences which de-schooling could not atone for:

> "Forcing someone to read can do lasting damage. If a child is allowed to learn at their own pace with no pressure, not only will they learn to read but they will enjoy it too."

This boy too had very bad experiences in school. He was also 11 at the time of the questionnaire:

> 75M: "Now home educated after years of bullying. It took us less than twenty minutes from finding out that home education was legal to having the de-reg letter written out. He has been home educated for 18 months. [He] is also SEN with we believe Dyspraxia, Dyslexia and visual processing disorder."

As in the example above, no attempts were made to teach him at home:

> "We did not specifically set out to teach him. We found that he was to all intents and purposes terrified /phobic about reading, convincing himself, after years of negative comments that he was unable to read. … We taught him, by not teaching him. We totally left reading

out of the equation for a whole year we occasionally dipped into it to find out what his feelings were towards reading, but we read to him every night and always pointed out signs and menus etc. His reading age shot up from our estimate of 5 or 6 years to age 10 in that year."

This young woman, who went on to higher education, was taken out of school aged 8:

66F: "[She] left school completely unable to read or spell even her own name. She was said to have dyseidetic and dysphonetic dyslexia, ADHD and dyspraxia. She had no word attack skills at all. Her reading ability was said to be in the bottom 3%."

At home the mother made no attempts to teach her daughter to read but concentrated instead on "facilitating her education, encouraging a return of a love of words and stories" and exercising her "patience in waiting till she was ready!"

She began to read as a teenager, aged 14, and "loves reading novels now."

These stories make remarkable reading. From them it is clear that what may begin as a difficulty in one area can spread into a much wider pool of consequences including severe emotional and mental trauma. The anxiety caused by reading difficulties can be severe and it is a moot point as to where school expectations might be said to cross a reasonable line between solving and creating problems.

As a result of the emotional repercussions of their school experiences parents were more concerned with addressing their children's general wellbeing than their educational problems. In each case the parents' tactics were to put reading on one side to concentrate on other aspects of education and to attend to their children's overall happiness and welfare. The strategy of leaving children with reading difficulties without instruction or regular reading practice is something unheard of in school and would no doubt be seen as highly neglectful. School strategies are always interventionist and children who are not meeting objectives are subject to greater and greater levels of concern and management designed to specifically identify and address problems. Programmes such as reading recovery for instance give intensive daily and individual lessons to children falling behind their school targets. The practices of the home educating parents offer a completely different approach to reading difficulties.

All three of these children became successful readers in the long term although, sadly, the pleasure of reading continued to elude one of the boys. Nevertheless, this level of attainment is remarkable. Falling behind in reading at school is a very serious situation. Once ground is lost in the mainstream it is rarely recovered. Poor reading almost always marks the beginning of the road into the educational wilderness from which most in that position will never return (McMillan and Leslie 1998). Certainly to move from the bottom 3% to being a college student who reads novels for pleasure is a rare story and one which home education should celebrate. Accounts like these three provoke questions about some of the realities of schooling but also about the possibilities and pathways which exist within education but to which perhaps insufficient mainstream attention has yet been paid.

Chapter Eleven

Matters of motivation

The role of motivation in learning to read

Many parents commented on the importance of children's own motivation to begin and follow through their explorations of reading. The importance of self-motivation ties in with the emphasis placed on child-led and child-paced learning, as discussed in Chapter Eight. Levels and directions of child motivation will set both the pace and the nature of literacy explorations and learning. Many parents saw the motivation to read as part and parcel of children's innate desires to explore their world and to imitate and join in with those around them. Parents characterised children as being naturally curious and naturally inclined to investigate their environment. Where this environment is a literate one, children will inevitably come across the written word:

> 12Fam: "Living life in a world where words are everywhere."
>
> 19Fam: "Our house is full of books, (we call it homeschooler insulation)."
>
> 7Fam: "We had books, magazines, newspapers, books on tape, books on CD, in our home, car, bedrooms, family and living rooms... bathrooms ...."

In addition, parents talked about motivation emanating from children's desire to join in the cultural world of those around them and to participate in their on-going activities:

> 8Fam: "seeing adults read"
>
> 36M: [he had] "a strong desire to look up information independently. Perhaps because he has always seen me study products, read books and magazines, information on the Internet."
>
> 54M: "Both my husband and I are avid readers. From us he has learned that reading is a way of gaining

information/answering questions as well as of relaxing."

56F: "Her cousins showing what they can read has occasionally motivated her."

79M: "They have a strong desire to read – particularly if reading is seen to be a highly valued skill in their family"

Barbara Rogoff in her cross cultural work on learning cites children's powers of observation and their attention to on-going events as being a key component in their learning (Rogoff, 1990). De Waal also notes the cross cultural tendency to "fit in" and the "desire to be like others" (de Waal, 2001, p 230 quoted in Lancy, 2014, p 158). The emphasis again lies on autonomy of action driven by social imperatives. Thus the dove-tailing of innate motivation with a literate environment creates a situation in which learning to read appears as an inevitable unfolding; the situation is no longer conducive but impelling. In such views internal motivation to adopt a cultural practice makes children autonomous learners with a high degree of natural independence yet set within a structure of cultural subject matter:

16F: "If they are surrounded by it they will want to do it."

20F: "In the presence of a rich language environment where the printed word is present and used, children come to reading on their own."

It seems that the elements of innate motivation, on-going social practice and facilitating environment combine together to form a powerful and apparently dependable imperative. Given this, time scales become of diminishing importance; individual variation is superseded in importance by the strength of both innate and cultural forces. Within a literate environment, children will inevitably become attracted to reading or as this parent put it:

41M: "You don't need to hurry the process, because they will get interested in learning how to read."

However, across the data motivation to read was not an

homogenous element and precisely what was motivating children was a matter subject to variation as was how that motivation manifested into action.

General motivation

Sometimes the spur to read came from a specific motivation in which the idea of reading itself had caught children's imagination. These parents reported a general desire to be able to read:

> 4F: "At 6 she decided she was ready to read books."
>
> 8M: "My son chose to read when it suited his need to read."
>
> 40F: "I think she was very interested in books and stories."
>
> 32Fam: "If they are surrounded by information they want to acquire … it motivates them to learn to read."

One of the two home educated adults who responded about themselves reflected on his desire to be able to read as an enabling life tool:

> 38M: "I got tired of asking what things said. … "

Specific motivation

Sometimes the desire to read was very specific; children wanted to be able to read a particular text for a particular purpose:

> 22F: "just being so interested in a story she heard that she wanted to read it herself."
>
> 41Fam: "Her desire to read materials pertaining to her interest."
>
> 10Fam: "When there was information they really wanted to get, that motivated them to learn."
>
> 8Fam: "Feeling the need inside themselves for either information or curiosity/enjoyment."
>
> 31M: "He is motivated by a desire to read words on things that interest him."

> 60F: "wanting to find out how something worked so instructions had to be read."

Once children had picked up on the idea of 'learning to read' many parents saw reading progress manifesting itself in terms of a self-motivated learning process. Thus there appeared to be a close relationship between motivation on the one hand and reading competence on the other; highly motivated children were able to use that motivation to jump start their reading, often very quickly:

> 37M: "It's truly by virtue of his own desire to 'crack the code'."

> 81M: "He needed to find a reason to want to read. We started playing World of Warcraft and he found his reason."

> 29M: "He decided that he wanted to read all of the Calvin and Hobbes comic books on his own. I helped him with the some of the bigger words (or helped him look up their definition), but he did the rest."

However, being able to read and wanting to read are not the same thing. Some children appeared to be able to read but were unmotivated to do so. This could have been because the balance between the effort required and the satisfaction achieved did not make reading worthwhile:

> 19Fam: "My son, while able to read most things, will SAY he can't read something if he is worried about it being difficult."

> 60F: [At what age would you say your child became able to read?]: "8/9 willingly"

> 29F: [what sort of things is your child interested in reading?] "Not much at the moment"

For other children choosing not to read (at least in certain situations) might be a more complicated, emotional choice or display of independence as the following quote seems to suggest:

> 56F: "She is very reluctant to tell people she has begun to read however – this I think is partly because she likes having

secrets but mainly because she is afraid it will be made a lot of..."

The kinds of comments quoted above indicate that parents sometimes could not tell what their child could do but only what their child wanted to do. In some cases, separating reading ability from feelings about reading was just not possible. Once again this indicates the holistic nature of learning to read in which emotion, context and participation are telling factors. Personal feelings, character traits, environmental factors all appear as possible elements in reading and are displayed throughout the data from loss of confidence in school (Chapter Ten) to high levels of enthusiasm to get information or join in particular activities.

Which comes first...?

Thus far, parents who are following models of child led, child paced learning are apparently dependent on children's own motivation to begin moves towards reading. They may proffer ideas: activities, games, drawing attention to the written word or to words in general, but if children do not pick up on the openings offered the parent has little option but to continue waiting. The emphasis on motivation begs the question of what happens if a child simply does not want to read. Many of the parents quoted above attest to the view that this will not happen. Children's natural curiosity and desire to join in will eventually lead them to reading. However, there were cases in which the things that parents said seemed to suggest a slightly different course.

The following quotes are about children who appear not to be motivated to read, and for good reason; for them at the moment it is a high effort, low reward activity:

> 36Fam: "The things that interest him are either too long and he feels intimidated by the length or the print is too small. He has difficulty following the small print."
>
> 29F: "She likes the idea of it but then gets fed up when she gets stuck on a word."

27M: "When I tried to get him to read it was so effortful that there was nothing in it for him to read something like *The Cat in the Ha*t. He seemed happy not to read – it didn't bother him he couldn't."

53M: "He is very capable however he would rather be read to".

Of course, given time, these children might well become motivated in the kind of general or specific way discussed above. Intriguingly however, some of the responses seemed to be hinting at a different interpretation. These stories seem to touch on different ideas about motivation; that motivation may be something that follows rather than leads learning:

19M: "I think one thing that really propelled him to read was wanting to find out what happened next in an exciting story but I was too tired to continue reading aloud. This was definitely how he ended up reading *The Hobbit* and *The Lord of the Rings* on his own."

52M: "Sometimes we had to tell him that we could not do that immediately because we were cooking dinner, for example. We would offer to read it as soon as practicable but one day after this, he said, "Fine, I'll just read it myself." A day or so later he could and did."

18M: "I got some early readers and when we used them he quickly said 'reading is boring'. I stopped immediately. Six months later he read by himself a Dr Seuss book *Green Eggs and Ham*. I could hear him one morning in his room."

6Fam: "My son started reading when he discovered the Harry Potter series."

In these examples children begin reading, sometimes at what would be considered a 'high' level, without having gone through the 'beginner' stage. This phenomenon was discussed in Chapter Six on learning trajectories where high ability seemed to suddenly emerge without a progressive rise. One way of considering this kind of trajectory might be through the idea of motivation. Instead of motivation leading to children learning, these children seem to be able to read and then become motivated to do so - by the time they want to read a particular text, they can. This can be seen as a reversal of the usual view of learning and its relation to motivation.

These two parents describe how reading had to be worthwhile before their children became motivated to engage in it:

> 27M: "When it became worthwhile for him in terms of what he could get out of it, then he started reading...before that all the effort he had to put into reading something very simple was just not worth it."

> 37Fam: "Like so many skills – it was having the mental capacity to do it almost effortlessly."

If some children are not motivated to read until they can read, we might consider this by returning to the idea that learning is natural. If learning is natural, in other words it is either a normal behaviour or the normal state of a healthy human being, then motivation may be considered irrelevant just as motivation to breath is irrelevant for a similarly healthy human. In this case what motivation might do is direct a child towards a particular activity or orientate them to a certain way of behaving but it does not direct their learning. In addition, the idea of 'reading' suggests a consciously recognised area of knowledge and a consciously held relationship to that area of knowledge. One parent called this mindful recognition, at least for her son, into question:

> 35M: "he doesn't see reading as separate from functioning on a day-to-day basis. If you were to ask him he would say he doesn't read because he perceives reading as sitting down with a book with lots of words."

This boy (7 at the time of the questionnaire) had learned to read on his own and as his mother pointed out, what he was learning had never been called anything in particular. There had been no separation between reading and any of the other things that he did or saw around him.

Understanding learning in this way is precluded from formal education in which knowing what is being learned is of vital importance to both teacher and student and learning objectives are an intrinsic part of good teaching. Indeed, it is largely precluded from a culture inclined to put so much emphasis on the act of learning, in which outlining the subject matter, demonstrating, assessing and managing learning is taken as the evidence that learning is happening. However, without these things there may be no recognition of learning at all.

This speculation leads to a further question. Can children learn to read without knowing that that is what they are doing? Certainly some parents attested that they became aware their children could read although they had observed no discernible process. Given how, in some cases, like the boy above, reading was a seamless aspect of life it seems equally possible that children do not realise this is what they are learning until the capability is revealed to them. Rather than learning how to read, children simply discover that they can:

> 58M: "You can't help but pick it up."

> 12F: "They won't be able to help themselves."

Or as the story of this boy is recounted:

> 4M: "He says "One day I just opened a book, thought I'd try and read it. It was about King Arthur I just read it, just like that. It felt good. I read a lot now. I think it's fun."

Such accounts stand in contrast to the usual depiction of learning as a concentrated and managed effort towards a pre-decided outcome. Yet logically for child led learning it makes sense that adult ends cannot be the goal of learning even if sometimes adult goals are fulfilled. I have explored some of these thoughts further in ideas about complex self-organisation (Pattison 2015) and turn now and finally to an exploration of complexity and the possibilities for understanding learning to read which its ideas offer.

Chapter Twelve

Considering learning to read through ideas of complexity

The established pattern of research is to seek out unifying strands within the subjects of its inquiry. Understanding is sought through the extraction of commonality so that experience can be generalised from the unique circumstances of an individual life or situation to a shared core of essential meaning. This is certainly the stance taken by reading research which aims to normalise the experience of learning to read by normalising the process and thence the procedure of learning to read. There are obvious reasons for this in a schooling system which has been pushing towards standardisation throughout its history. This research however takes the debate in a different direction.

The vast majority of children in this research had learned to read successfully; other parents did not (yet) see their children as 'readers' but were able to indicate aspects of their children's relationship to literacy. But there the commonality within the sample seems to end. Children learned at different ages, in different ways, through different experiences, within different family philosophies and approaches to reading and forged for themselves varied kinds of relationships to the written word. The contexts of their reading were varied within multiple dimensions; their experiences diverse and unique.

Constructing ideas about learning to read

In educational terms reading is overwhelmingly regarded as a 'cognitive skill'. Its designation as such has much to do with the highly influential work of Keith Stanovich who through the course of the 1980s and 1990s produced a stream of extremely influential papers which continue to form the backbone of much of our understanding of reading (Coles 2000). The categorising of reading in this way has particular philosophical implications for how we understand what reading is and from there considerable influence on how we understand it to be learned. *The Oxford*

Dictionary of Psychology defines cognition as "the mental activities involved in acquiring and processing information" (Colman 2009 online no page numbers). Using this definition, the logical, perhaps only way, to understand reading is as an interior mental act in which knowledge of a system is 'acquired' and is then internally 'processed' by the reader. The designation of reading as a 'skill' similarly lays out a particular path of understanding whilst simultaneously foreclosing other possibilities. As Blake *et al* argue "skills relate to means whose ends are predetermined" (Blake *et al*, 2000, p26) and as they go on "there is something limited and limiting about a conception of learning that makes it essentially a matter of skills acquisition" (Blake *et al*, 2000, p26). Certainly this might be well illustrated by the demonstration of reading 'skills' through the 'de-coding' of pseudo words. Through the representation of reading as a 'cognitive skill' then the site for a very particular and mechanistic approach to reading is cleared, bringing with it huge implications for reading education.

The skills approach to reading bestows equally a clear logic on the subskills breakdown methodology which governs reading education. By this means structural features of reading can be identified and used across data on children's reading prowess to create analytical patterns and meaning (Haggis, 2008). Such structural features however are not self-evident; they have to be named and established and in doing so categorised as to their contribution to the overall 'skill'. The establishment of the key role of phonemic awareness is one such obvious example (Stanovich 1994) but even in socio-cultural arguments such features can also be cited; for example, the emphasis placed on reading aloud to children.

The creation of these kinds of structural feature has a twofold effect. Firstly, the individuality of experience is broken up. This was illustrated in Chapter Five where it was shown that 'reading to children' could be enacted quite differently between families and could equally be endowed with different ideas about its contribution. In theories that present 'reading to children' as a single category this variation becomes homogenised under one understanding. Secondly the flow of experience is broken up such that an event will either belong within a category or not. The difficulties of this approach were also illustrated in Chapter Four in which what counted as teaching was questioned. Theories resting on categorisation are forced to designate, for example, particular actions as teaching or not teaching without being able to encompass the kind of inherent uncertainty uncovered through parents' accounts and presented here. Bundling data together into homogenous categories, argues Haggis (2008), masks important information including the differences between experiences, the contexts of experiences and the relevance of both time and process as well as other aspects of the phenomena which have not been used as the organising principle. Things which are not of the same nature, things which might be carried out with different intentions and meanings or in different circumstances and relationships are nevertheless put together in categories as if they are the same thing (Foucault 1970).

Once these kinds of homogenous categories have been created, cause and effect links can be put into place that structure how we understand reading. These links can then also be used as explanations as to why children are or are not reading for themselves. For example, in his book *The Meaning Makers* (1986), Gordon Wells, discusses the fate of Rosie, a child in his study who is not read to at home. He argues that this constitutes a "serious deficiency" (Wells, 1986, p169) in Rosie's reading education which is not atoned for in school. The direct result of this, he goes on, is that Rosie's schooling becomes a sad tale of minimal progress and the prospect of a grim future ahead of her. In this argument reading is an effect which results from causes, a major one of which is being read to. Where this cause is missing, the desired effect cannot be achieved. Similar arguments are deployed in relation to phonemic awareness, for example by Goswami (2009). Levels of phonemic awareness are used to explain differences in reading success in an argument which makes phonemic awareness a contributory cause of the effect of reading.

Cause and effect linkages support teaching theories and socio-cultural theories alike, inhabiting both the metaphors of participation and acquisition. A cause is implemented, whether deliberately or accidentally, leading to an effect which can then be understood in terms of its causes. Reading can be seen as an effect which arises through a particular cause or number of causes. By this means educational thinking can not only look backwards with understanding but also look forwards with deliberation. Phonemic awareness, being read to, living in a literate environment can all be designated as causes of reading. Once this link is theoretically established the provision of causes can be made deliberate and systematic, some may be designated further as teaching and a system or procedure for learning to read can be created.

To question this kind of educational thinking requires that we question the cause and effect links on which it is premised. Coles (2000) in his critique of much of the research underlying phonics theories of learning to read questions the causation links between phonemic awareness and reading. He argues that insufficient work has been done to eliminate the possibility that proficient reading enables children to 'do' phonics rather than the other way around. In other words, the direction of causality may be reversed. Here however, I want to raise the concern that the particular logic inherent in cause and effect understandings is itself merely a way of thinking about the world; one of a number of different possible means of understanding how one thing may affect another.

The logic of cause and effect which has guided thinking in both the sciences and social sciences for so long is coming now under increasing pressure. In recent times the straight forward linear thinking associated with cause and effect has been disrupted in at least two ways. Firstly, the post-modern turn of thought has postulated that thought cannot be disassociated from its thinker; all understanding is contextualised and therefore the logical world of cause and effect should be understood as the particular perspective of certain historical and cultural groups, rather than as a given way in which the world works.

> "It is not possible to detect a cause empirically or prove that one exists philosophically. We can never directly sense a cause. We merely induce their existence from our own experience of the association of two or more events, and this is nothing more than a habit of mind – immutable though it appears… our notion of cause is little more than a superstition" (Gorard, 2000, p 3-4).

Amongst the implications of this disruption to our accepted ways of thinking is that all- encompassing theories, including those of education, are no longer possible (Lather, 1991). Post modernism gives permission for us to think about children learning to read away from the ideas of cause and effect. One possible and relatively new way of thinking about the ways in which what appear to be discrete phenomena are or may become inter connected is through the forms of association suggested by the ideas of chaos and complexity. These ideas do not dis-clude notions of cause and effect but they do alter their premises and in so doing provide us with our second interruption to linearity.

Complexity

Chaos, and its off shoot complexity, are branches of scientific thinking which have been emerging steadily through the last half of the 20th century and are now in the process of making their way across to the social science agenda. During the 1970s a scattering of intellectual pioneers across the range of the natural sciences found themselves increasingly pushing against the limits of classically ordered science; the cause and effect kind of regularity that had been being built on since Newton (Gleick, 1987). One of the reasons behind this push was the problem of enclosed systems. The scientific ideal of pristine and sealed laboratory conditions were clearly unobtainable in the 'real' world and caused a constant stumbling block in transferring theory to practice in fields from economics to meteorology. Chaos theory is based on the alternative foundation that insufficiency of information always means that starting conditions can never be fully established and therefore, even in theory, never held constant. Taylor (2001) cites two reasons for this inability. Firstly, that systems are not bounded wholes but are necessarily open and therefore can never be considered complete. Secondly that systems involve "recursive relations" (Taylor, 2001, p 24) which generate feed-back and feed forward loops which confound linearity. The consequence of this is that systems are unstable and unpredictable over anything other than the extremely short term.

A further implication is that the possibility of understanding situations or systems by examining what appear to be their components is precluded. Chaos postulates that systems are based not on discrete constituents but on the interrelationships between constituents which by virtue of their reciprocal relations are not stable such that "the collectivity possesses properties and energies not possessed by the parts, but through which change can take place, new forms and patterns can develop" (Olssen, 2008, p 103). There is a constant and dynamic interaction between the elements of such a system and between the system and the environment in which it is located. This interaction cannot be understood by unpicking parts within it because parts cannot be meaningfully extracted from the whole. Indeed, such a method of analysis, argues Cilliers, "destroys what it seeks to understand" (Cilliers, 1998, p 2), An holistic grasp of interrelationships is necessary to address complex systems.

Complex self-organising systems

Complexity theory, emerged from chaos theory founded on the same premise that "in a system there are more possibilities than can be actualised" (Cilliers, 1998, p2). However, complexity theory focuses on the borderlands between order and disorder. What makes this space between order and chaos a system, rather than a jumble of myriad and unpredictable factors is self-organisation. In the border land between "too much and too little order ...self-organizing systems emerge to create new patterns of coherence and structures of relation" (Taylor, 2001, p 24/25). Self-organising systems are not the result of prior design but are a constantly changing emergent and adapting dynamic which depends neither on "the intervention of an external designer or the presence of some centralised form of internal control" (Cilliers, 1998, p 89). Complexity aims to acknowledge the dynamics of interaction and the non-linear nature of systems both in terms of the system itself and the interaction between that system and the environment in which it is located (Cilliers, 1998). Self-organisation is an emergent property generated from within the system as a result of "complex interaction between the environment, the present state of the system and the history of the system" (Cilliers, 1998, p 89).

Such arrangements are not simply reactive or sensitive to their environment but are active, increasing in complexity over time and tending towards "a critical point between rigid order and chaos" (Cilliers, 1998, p 97). At this point, flexibility is at its optimum with the system being neither too rigid nor too disorganised to respond to change appropriately whether that change is an influence outside the system or a reorganisation within the system.

Complex systems, Cilliers argues, are, for the most part, living systems with "the human brain [being] considered by many to be the most complex object known" (Cilliers, 1998, p5). Like all complex systems, it has the capacity "to develop or change internal structure spontaneously and adaptively in order to cope with or manipulate the environment" (Cilliers, 1998, p 90). Each human brain forms a complex, self-organising system so that even for those living in the same environment organisation is idiosyncratic and varied and not dependant on the inclusion of particular parts. Rather than a structure which can be seen as shared or as a constant across similar systems there are myriad, variable systems which do not necessarily contain the same elements, let alone the same elements in the same order. Information is related to other information in "relationships [that] are not fixed, but shift and change, often as a result of self-organisation. This can result in novel features, usually referred to in terms of emergent properties" (Cilliers, 1998, p viii - ix).

Applying the insights of complexity theory to an understanding of children learning to read appears to be not only suitable in terms of the theory's own remit but offers the opportunity to consider the home education data in ways which, unlike traditional forms of analysis, is able to preserve the individuality stressed by parents and the unique configurations found in the data itself. In the case of each individual child, reading can be considered as a property emerging through the dynamic self-organisation of the relationships between the environment, the history of the child and the on-going organisation of the system itself.

Applying the ideas of complexity to reading data

The ideas of complexity have not been applied before in reading research yet some similar strands of thinking are discernible in some of the things which parents said.

Possibilities rather than prescriptions

> 44Fam: "It was only after the younger child was reading fluently that I realized that I'd neglected to first teach her the alphabet song ... she did eventually learn the alphabet song (although not very well) ... "knowing the alphabet" is clearly not an essential "pre-reading skill"!"

> 26M: "The idea of a reductionist approach to reading (e.g. you must learn the alphabet etc) does not hold much weight with us."

> 7Fam: "We had phonics books in the home, some flashcards available, but they didn't seem his thing... phonics had nothing to do with any of my kids' abilities"

> 23Fam: "He has never let me read to him"

In these quotes, the parent's comments illustrate how no one particular designated feature is essential to learning to read. In the first case, the parent points out that knowing the alphabet is not critical to learning to read. The same could be applied to other 'essential' criteria such as being read to or the development of phonemic awareness. In this argument rather than specific sub skills being pre-requisites onto which further pre-set skills can be built, interaction occurs between what is available at any given state of the system allowing for the creation of endless idiosyncratic possibilities. It is the recursive and on-going relationships between, and interrelation of, parts within the system which allows for reading to emerge, rather than the fulfilling of pre-given criteria.

Dynamic systems

> 31M: "I have decided not to pursue a formal approach because my son appears to learn more happily and more concretely by pursuing his own interests and timetable. I have no doubt that he will learn to read."

> 26M: "The development of reading skills may turn out to be a chaotic (in the physics sense of the word) process... child development is a dynamic, creative process and requires support rather than control."

These parent's remarks could be taken to be illustrative of the dynamism of self-organising systems in which the child's own interests and timing can lead to connections and coherence through unique configurations that make sense of a child's own perspective and experience. The parent's difficulty in following a formal course can be seen as indicative of the difficulties inherent in predicting the course of complex systems. In such a view of reading "knowledge accumulates in unpredictable ways and its practical consequences are unforeseeable" (Brown, 2002, p 27) and this may be as true for the child who is learning as it is for observers. Thus, in the light of self-organisation, it would be more than possible for a child to learn to read, not through the pursuit of reading (either their own or an externally managed process), but through the dynamic interrelationship of any number of factors individual and idiosyncratic to them, muddled together in no particular order and according to no linear idea of progress nor to any time scale (Pattison, 2015).

Organisation rather than accumulation

> 32 Fam: "The process was not continuous. There was a week or some weeks when reading and writing or the interest on the subject was very intense and then there was no interest for weeks or months. But when they started to be interested again I always noticed that there has been something happening in between ... they made connections which they didn't do before or there was just more knowledge than before."

> 44F: "One day she could recognise letters and their sounds but couldn't sound out words and the next she was reading road signs to me and reading quite complicated words by herself. She learned very quickly after that and was very fluent almost at once. I was amazed by her ability and by how quickly it developed. ... I really feel that something seemed to change within her - one day she couldn't read and then she could, it was really that sudden."

That a self-organising system could be at work would help to explain how such an apparently fallow period might be followed by an unexpected leap forward. The system of understanding is not reliant on more and more input in the way that a transmission of skills theory is; instead it is the on-going organisation of what is already in the system that makes the difference. Self-organisation allows for change to occur not solely through the accumulation of elements but rather the organisation of those elements, a process not subject to a predictable time scale or to external control. As the self-organising system is not under conscious or central control, it would not be recognisable to the learner him or herself or presumably to any observer as a form of effort.

Metaphors of osmosis

This work has been much concerned with metaphors and the understandings which emanate from them. Some parents employed unusual metaphors themselves, one such being that of osmosis.

Osmosis is the tendency of the molecules of a solvent to pass through a semi-permeable membrane from a less concentrated solution to a more concentrated one. This biological description was used by some parents as a metaphor for the assimilation of literacy:

> 16Fam: "The whole process of learning to read by virtual osmosis is amazing."
>
> 39Fam: "[He] seems to have learned by osmosis."

The metaphor of osmosis depicts the passage of literacy from the environment to the individual. It simultaneously postulates the adaptation of the individual to the environment leading to both changes in the environment and the individual. In this the metaphor encompasses elements of both ideas of acquisition and participation. The osmosis metaphor also conveys the idea that literacy is a liquid and therefore that learning to read is both a fluid and a natural phenomenon; a series of entailments which seems to suit the perspectives of home educators rather well.

Osmosis occurs naturally because of the juxtaposition of two substances. It does not involve effort, volition or awareness. It is a purely physical reaction shared by organisms with and without conscious minds. The interface between the two substances needs to be one receptive to a transference but there is no requirement for a third party to mediate, control or facilitate the transference.

Similar metaphors have been used in discussions of self-organising systems. For example, Taylor employs the word 'screen' to discuss the work of the human mind. He describes a filtering system which is "like a permeable membrane ... it does not simply divide but also joins by simultaneously keeping out and letting through" (Taylor, 2003, p 199). The screening of information, like the screening of osmosis allows some things to mix but not others; a selection of the meaningful and a rejection of what is not. This filtering system without central control or explicit purpose is a self-organising system which sorts and selects in dynamic ways and which can (at least sometimes) be articulated into knowledge as we understand it. The same point might be more simply put as:

21F: "They will learn to read in the way that best fits them."

Open systems

Complex systems are open systems; they have no boundaries. This is both in terms of their historical antecedents and in terms of their current elements of potential influence. As far as learning to read is concerned this means that every experience, past or present in a child's life is an actual or potential contributor to their relationship to literacy.

35M: "Learning to read is easy when children can do so in their own time, at their own pace and without it being called anything in particular."

In this quote an open system is being hinted at. Reading is not enclosed by the kind of definition which would enable us to call it something in particular, including its breaking down into subparts. In other words, the range of experience which might play into a reader's relationship with the written word is unlimited in the same way in which complex systems are seen as unbounded and always incomplete.

47M: "He wanted to learn the lyrics to his favourite CD. He sat with the lyrics and played the songs over and over, following the words on the page and singing along."

For this boy, his favourite CD and his interest in singing are retrospectively recognisable influences in his learning to read. But they are not elements in a system which can be recognised as such, away from the child who has used them in a particular way to satisfy his own particular ends.

By its very nature, such a view of learning to read cannot be pre-arranged or organised; but only experienced. In such a model, both parents and children are agents whose behaviour is contingent on, and emergent from, the system as they experience it. The way in which parents talked about helping their children can be seen as emerging from such a system, dependent on and formed by their own and their children's changing ideas:

> 10F: "We helped when asked"
>
> 22F: "I did help when asked."
>
> 24F: "Anything she asked, I helped her with."
>
> 55F: "I can't say I really taught her. She wanted my help, so I gave it."
>
> 71M: "[He asked] for help as and when needed."

Of course much that might be seen as 'help' from a transmission perspective would not be recognised as such by either parents or children. It would simply be interaction or elements which might or might not enter the self-organising system with significance. This is then the antithesis of a system in which inputs lead to outcomes. Indeed, there is no 'outcome' as such, the system simply continues to evolve and emerge. Parents echoed this view when they talked about learning to read as a natural process following its own apparent course and about the feeling sometimes that when they had intervened with intent they had actually disrupted some other unsuspected and unseen process. These views are expressed in the section on teaching in which parents questioned their own understanding of what teaching can achieve:

> 36Fam: "ultimately she learned at her own pace and on her own. I feel I interfered with her natural process."

This is not to say that what might be seen as teaching, or some other form of mediation is not a possibility as a contributory factor in learning to read. According to the above it must be and must have, at least potentially, as many possibilities for inclusion and influence as any other available element, however, its central characterisation as intentional and directional would no longer be possible.

Employing the ideas of complexity with which to address

learning to read at home leads to some provocative inferences. Through the lens of complexity, the idea of a best, or only, method of learning to read is finally expunged. Equally the concern that there is an optimum age of learning beyond which children who are not reading have a problem can be logically disputed. Thirdly it has an intrinsic appeal when so many of the home educating parents, both collectively and individually, present insights and arguments that fit so well into the frame of complexity. Above all this research has uncovered and confirmed the collective difference to which individual home educators have testified. This difference has been expressed in many ways; from the terms in which reading is understood to the insistence of parents on the uniqueness of each child and of each child' experience. Complexity offers a way of holding onto this diversity without sacrificing understanding to it. The implications of this for formal schooling are far-reaching and difficult; the possibilities for informal learning, vast and exciting.

Continuing

Most research ends with a conclusion. This research chooses not to. There have been too many conclusions drawn about reading already. This research instead has attempted to open and re-open questions about what reading is, what learning is, how we understand these things and what new ideas might be applied to probe and challenge these understandings in pertinent and invigorating ways. Home education offers important ground on which to consider these questions and to ponder on new and different lines of thought that could be fruitfully developed. Like the self-organising systems described above, re-thinking learning to read should, and should be allowed to, continue evolving, emerging, changing and developing. Conclusions close inquiry down; re-thinking aims to open them up and in this spirit I offer this exploration forward.

Afterword

There is a long tradition of research being seen as a neutral activity in which dispassionate people set out to discover the truth about certain aspects of the world or to answer questions with a scientific rigour and method that is unaffected by the political and cultural context of their work. In the postmodern world, however, this view is becoming less and less acceptable. The role that politics and culture play, as well as researchers' own interests in their subject matter, are increasingly recognized as factors in the kind of questions which research asks and the kind of knowledge which it is able to produce. This recognition has led to the idea that rather than there being single truths which will lead us inexorably in the direction of progress we should be able to accept and indeed embrace the idea that the exploration of life may be carried out through a diversity of narratives and frames of understanding.

It is tempting to see such ideals as providing the umbrella under which alternative views of education may find some degree of official recognition and legitimacy. Usher and Edwards for example argue that post-modernism no longer validates the view of education as "a straitjacket of uniform provision, standardized curricular, technicised teaching methods and bearer of universal 'messages' of rationality and morality" (Usher and Edwards, 1994, p211). This may sound like a welcome endorsement of much that home educators have to offer in terms of practical examples of what can happen to learning away from the main stream as well as in theoretical and philosophical thought. However, unfortunately, in practice no such haven for alternative education has been forthcoming. According to Usher and Edwards, "education ... is particularly resistant to the postmodern 'message'" (Usher and Edwards, 1994, p1). This resistance has been and continues to be a significant feature of the political and cultural climate in which alternative education is practised and which has had its own bearing on the research which informs this book.

Yet despite the continual pull towards standardization, there seems little doubt that the global educational landscape is changing; the rise of home education is part of that change but the significance of now decades long expansion in alternative education is, as yet unclear. The force of the change however is perhaps indicated by its growth in an often suspicious and even hostile climate. Under circumstances in which home educators frequently feel threatened and even, at times, persecuted, research offers an opportunity to present evidence and mount arguments. As a political tool research can be seen as an engine of possibility; a way of telling how it really is, and of opening up the minds of decision making powers. Certainly from an ethical point of view if home education is to be made subject to tighter regulation then it is morally important that strenuous efforts be made to understand the educational practices and ideas which go on under its auspices.

The study of reading and the new perspectives which the home educators' experiences allow us has taken us beyond the questions of regulating, assessing and monitoring the learning of children who do not go to school. Instead it has much more dramatically and importantly opened up to question the philosophical heart of reading and learning. Educational thinking has long been committed to certain views of these things; views which have shaped discourse, research, policy and pedagogy. In these postmodern times we can no longer accept these things as reflections of an unassailable reality. Instead we are entering a new process of making meaning; meaning that will have far-reaching and long term consequences for unpredictably large numbers of children and their families. Whilst monitoring and regulation schemes will no doubt represent an important expression of this meaning, deciding what education is has far greater portent than acts of legislation.

The ethical implications of meaning have never been far from this research. Our commitment to a certain view of what it means to read has far reaching consequences. As Cilliers puts it, "since a certain theory of representation implies a certain theory of meaning – and meaning is what we live by – our choice of such a theory has important ethical implications" (Cilliers, 1998, p 88). Nowhere in the educational field can the moral burdens that accompany the laying out of such representations be heavier than in the matter of learning to read. The terms in which we establish what reading is, and our ideas about how children might come by it, have far reaching implications that impact on the lives of children and their families in almost every sense imaginable, from the practical to the emotional and continue to carry consequences that stretch far beyond the school years. We must, all of us, be ever mindful of this responsibility.

References

Abboud, S.K. and Kim, J. (2011) *Top of the Class: How Asian Parents Raise High Achievers--And How You Can Too* New York: Berkley Books

Antikainen, A (2007) *Transforming a Learning Society: The Case of Finland*. Peter Lang: Bern

Baker, J. (1964) *Children in Chancery*, London, Hutchinson

Badman, G (2009) *Report to the Secretary of State on the Review of Elective Home Education in England*. HC 610, London: TSO

BBC (2012) *Tips for Good Homework Habits* [online] www.bbc.co.uk/schools/parents/primary_support (accessed August 2012)

Bissex, G.L. (1980) *Gnys at work: A child learns to write and read*. Cambridge, MA: Harvard University Press.

Blake, N., Smeyers, P. Smith, R. and Standish, P. (2000) *Education in an Age of Nihilism*. London: Routledge

Blunden, A. (2004) *Sen on Participation* [online] ethicalpolitics.org/reviews/sen-particpation.htm (accessed May 2012)

Britton, J. (1983) Writing and the Story World. In Kroll, B. and Wells C. (eds) *Explorations in the Development of Writing*. Chichester: Wiley

Bruner, J. (1996) *The Culture of Education*. Massachusetts: Harvard University Press

Brown, K. (2002) *The Right to Learn*. London: Routledge

Browne, A. (2009) *Developing Language and Literacy 3 – 8*. London: Sage

Cilliers, P. (1998) *Complexity and Postmodernism*. London: Routledge

Clark, M. (1976) *Young Fluent Readers*. Oxford: Heinemann

Children Better Prepared For School If Their Parents Read Aloud to Them (2008) *British Medical Journal Science Daily* [online] www.sciencedaily.com/releases/2008/05/080512191126.htm (accessed August 2013)

Coles, G. (2000) *Misreading Reading: The Bad Science that Hurts Children*. Portsmouth: Heinemann

Colman, A. (2009) *The Oxford Dictionary of Psychology*. Oxford: Oxford University Press

Deleuze, G. and Guattari, F. (1987) *A Thousand Plateaus; Capitalism and Schizophrenia*. Minneapolis: Minnesota Press

Department for Children, Schools and Families (2009) *Morgan: action to ensure children's education & welfare* [on-line] webarchive.nationalarchives.gov.uk/20100204110606/http://www.dcsf.gov.uk/pns/DisplayPN.cgi?pn_id=2009_0013 (accessed April 2016)

Department for Education (2015) *Reading the Next Steps* [on-line] www.gov.uk/government/uploads/system/uploads/attachment_data/file/409409/Reading_the_next_steps.pdf (accessed April 2016)

Department for Education (2016) *2016 Key stage 1: Assessment and reporting arrangements* (ARA) Standards and Testing Agency [on-line] www.gov.uk/guidance/2016-key-stage-1-assessment-and-reporting-arrangements-ara/section-7-phonics-screening-check (accessed March 2016)

Department for Education (2012) *Statutory Framework for the Early Years Foundation Stage*. Runcorn: Department for Education.

Dhillon, A (2013) *Net Gains for 'Slum' Children*. In Hancock, R., Collins, J. and Stacey, M. (eds) *Primary Teaching Assistants Learners and Learning*. Oxford: Routledge

Dowty, T. (2000) *Free Range Education* Stroud: Hawthorn Press

Elliot, R. K. (1984) *Imagination and Conceptions of Education*. In Taylor, W. (ed) *Metaphors of Education*. London: Heinemann

Ferreiro, E. (1985) *Literacy Development*. In Olson, D., Torrance, N. and Hildyard, A. (eds) *Literacy, Language, and Learning*. Cambridge; Cambridge University Press

Fischer, S. R. (2003) *A History of Reading*. London: Reaktion Books

Fortune-Wood, M. (2009) *How to Home Educate. The Ecologist* [online] www.theecologist.org (accessed December 2011)

Foucault, M. (1970) *The Order of Things*. London: Tavistock Publications Ltd

Gee, J. P. (2009) *Literacy, Video Games, and Popular Culture*. In Olson, D. and Torrance, N. (eds.) *The Cambridge Handbook of Literacy*. Cambridge: Cambridge University Press

GHEC (2012) *Global Home Education Conference 2012*. 1 – 4 November, Berlin [on line]
www.ghec2012.org/cms/ (accessed May 2016)

Gleick, J. (1987) *Chaos*. London: Heinemann

Goswami, U. (2009) *The Basic Processes in Reading: Insights from Neuroscience*. In Olson, D. and Torrance, N. (eds.) *The Cambridge Handbook of Literacy*. Cambridge: Cambridge University Press

Graff, H. J. (1987) *The Labyrinths of Literacy*. Lewes: The Falmer Press

Graff, H.J. (1987) *The Legacies of Literacy*. Bloomington, Indiana University Press

Graff, H.J. Mackinnon, A., Sandin, B. and Winchester, I. (2009) Socio-cultural *History and the Legacy of Egil Johansson Introduction to Understanding Literacy in its Historical Contexts*, edited by the authors.

Gramley, S. (2011) *The History of English*: An Introduction. London: Routledge

Gorard, S. (2000) *The Role of Cause and Effect in Education as a Social Science*. ESRC Teaching and Learning Research Programme, Research Capacity Building Network, Occasional Paper Series, Paper 43 [online] www.tlrp.org/rcbn/capacity/Papers/Cause.pdf (accessed August 2012)

Haggis, T. (2008) *Knowledge must be contextual: Some Possible Implications of Complexity and Dynamic Systems Theories for Educational Research*. In Mason, M. (ed) *Complexity Theory and the Philosophy of Education*. Chichester: Wiley-Blackwell

Harris, R. (2009) *Speech and Writing*. In Olson, D. and Torrance, N. (eds.) *The Cambridge Handbook of Literacy*. Cambridge: Cambridge University Press

Harrison, J.E.C. (1988) *The Common People*, London, Fontana

Harrison, A (2011) *Reading check for six-year-olds rolled out*. BBC News 16 September [on-line] www.bbc.co.uk/news/education-14930193 (accessed May 2016)

Holt, G. (1984) *Metaphors in Science and Education*. In Taylor, W. (ed) *Metaphors of Education*. London: Heinemann

Illich, I. (1995) *De-schooling Society*. London: Marion Boyars Ltd

Jesson, R., McNaughton, S. and Kolose, T. (2014) *Investigating the summer learning effect in low SES schools* in *Australian Journal of Language and Literacy*. 37 (1)

Kunzman, R. (2009) *Write These Laws on your Children*. Massachusetts: Beacon Press

Lacqueur, T. (1976) *The cultural origin of popular literacy in England, 1500-1850* Oxford Review of Education, Vol 2, 255-275

Lakoff, G. and Johnson, M. (1980) *Metaphors We Live By*. London: University of Chicago Press

Lave, J. and Wenger, E. (1991) *Situated Learning: Legitimate Peripheral Participation*. Cambridge, Cambridge University Press

Lancy, D. (2014) *The Anthropology of Childhood*. Cambridge: Cambridge University Press

Lather, P. (1991) *Getting Smart: Feminist Research and Pedagogy With/in the Postmodern*. New York: Routledge

Lewis, I. M. (1985) *Social Anthropology in Perspective*. Cambridge: Cambridge University Press

Long, E. (2009) *Ways of Reading*. In Olson, D. and Torrance, N. (eds.) *The Cambridge Handbook of Literacy*. Cambridge: Cambridge University Press

McMillan, G. and Leslie, M. (1998) *Early Intervention Handbook: Intervention in Literacy*. Edinburgh: City of Edinburgh Council, Education Department

Meighan, R. (1997) *The Next Learning System*. Nottingham: Educational Heretics Press

Monk, D. (2009) *Regulating home education: negotiating standards, anomalies and rights*. In *Child and Family Law Quarterly*, 21, (2)

Morrow, L. M. (2012). *Literacy Development in the Early Years*. Boston: Pearson Education, Inc.

National Literacy Trust (2012) *Words for Life* [online] www.literacytrust.org.uk/ (accessed August 2012)

Nicholson, F. (2012) *Home Education Law in England* [online] Ed Yourself: The Home Education Consultancy. Available from: edyourself.org/articles/helaw.php (accessed August 2012)

Nicholson, F. (2016) *How many children are home educated in England?* [online] Ed Yourself: The Home Education Consultancy. Available from:
edyourself.org/articles/FAQ.php

Olssen, M. (2008) *Foucault as Complexity Theorist: Overcoming the Problems of Classical Philosophical Analysis.* In Mason, M. (ed.) *Complexity Theory and the Philosophy of Education.* Chichester: Wiley-Blackwell

Pattison, H. (2014) *Re-thinking Learning to Read – The challenge from children educated at home* PhD thesis University of Birmingham. Available from: http://etheses.bham.ac.uk/5051/

Pattison, H. (2015) *Complex Self-Organising Systems and the Unschooled Child.* New Research in Philosophy of Education Conference, University of Sheffield: UK

Pattison, H. (2016) *Education and the time of our lives.* In *Other Education Special Issue – Nihilism and Education* Peim, N. (ed)

Pattison, H. (in preparation) *Raising Literacy*: Reading as a Community Practice

Pattison, H. and Thomas, A. (2016) *Great Expectations: Agenda and Authority in Technological, Hidden and Cultural Curriculums in Lees,* H and Noddings, N. (eds) *The Palgrave International Handbook of Alternative Education.* London: Palgrave Macmillan

Peim, N and Flint, K (2009) *Testing Times: Questions concerning assessment for school improvement in Educational Philosophy and Theory* 41 (3)

Penketh, C. (2014) *Invention and repair: disability and education after the UK Coalition Government.* In *Disability & Society,* 29 (9)

Petrie, A., Windrass, G. & Thomas, A. (1998) *Prevalence of Home Education in England: a Feasibility Study.* DfES Research Report

Popkewitz, T. (1987). *The Formation of the School Subjects.* London: The Falmer Press.

Prins, E and Toso, B. W. (2008) *Defining and Measuring Parenting for Educational Success: A Critical Discourse Analysis of the Parent Education Profile.* American Educational Research Journal, 45 (3), 555 - 596

Reddy, M. (1978) *The Conduit Metaphor: A case of frame conflict in our language about language*. In Ortoney, A. (ed) *Metaphor and Thought*. Cambridge: Cambridge University Press

Rogoff, B. (1990) *Apprenticeship in Thinking*. New York: Oxford University Press

Rogoff B (1994) *Developing understanding of the idea of communities of learners*. In *Mind, Culture and Activity* 1:4 209 – 229

Rothermel, P. (2015) *Introduction*. In Rothermel, P. (ed) *International Perspectives on Home Education* Hants: Palgrave Macmillan

Sfard, A. (1988) *On Two Metaphors for Learning and the Dangers of Choosing Just One*. Educational Researcher 27 (4)

Slavin, R., Lake, C., Davis, S., Madden, N. (2009) *What Works for Struggling Readers*. University of York, Institute for Effective Education www.bestevidence.org.uk/assets/what_works_for_struggling_readers.pdf (Accessed February 2014)

Smith, F. (1997) *Reading Without Nonsense*. New York: Teachers College Press

Smith, F (2004) *Understanding Reading*. London: Routledge

Stainthorp, R and Hughes D, (1999) *Learning from Children who Read at an Early Age*. London: Routledge

Stake, R. E. (2000) *The Case Study Method in Social Inquiry*. In Gomm, R., Hammersley, M. and Foster, P. (eds) *Case Study Method*. London: Sage

Stanovich, K. (1993) *Romance and reality The Reading Teacher* 47 (4)

Suissa, J. (2006) *Untangling the Mother Knot: Some Thoughts on Parents, Children and Philosophers of Education. Ethics and Education*. 1, 65 – 77

Taylor, M. (2001) *The Moment of Complexity*. Chicago: The University of Chicago Press

Terzi, L. (2010) *Justice and Equality in Education – A Capability Perspective on Disability and Special Educational Needs*. London: Continuum.

Thomas, A. (1998) *Educating Children at Home*. London: Continuum

Thomas, A and Pattison, H (2007) *How Children Learn at Home*.

London: Continuum

Thomas, A and Pattison, H (2013) *Informal Home Education; Philosophical Aspirations put into Practice in Studies* in *Philosophy and Education* 32 (2)

Tizard, B. and Hughes, M. (1984) *Young Children learning at Home and in School*. London: Fontana

Torgeson, J. (1998) *Catch Them before They Fall: Identification and Assessment To Prevent Reading Failure in Young Children*. American Educator, 22 (1)

Trevarthen, C. (1995) *The Child's Need to Learn a Culture*. In Woodhead, M. Falukner, D. and Littleton, K. (eds) *Cultural Worlds of Early Childhood*. London: Routledge

Tsabar, B. (2014) *Resistance and Imperfection as Educational Work: Going against the 'Harmony' of Individualistic Ideology*. Other Education, 3 (1)

UNESCO *Education for All* (EFA) (2006) *Education for All Global Monitoring Report, Literacy for Life* [online] www.unesco.org/new/en/education/themes/leading-the-international-agenda/efareport/ (accessed July 2012)

US Department of Education, (2012) *Table 206.10 Number and Percentage of home schooled students ages 5 through 17 with a grade equivalent of kindergarten through 12th grade by selected child, parent and household characteristics*: 2003, 2007 and 2012 [on line] https://nces.ed.gov/programs/digest/d13/tables/dt13_206.10.asp?current=yes (accessed April 2016)

Usher, R. and Edwards, R. (1994) *Post Modernism and Education Different Voices, Different Worlds*. London: Routledge

Weinberger, J. (1996) *Literacy goes to School*. London: Paul Chapman Publishing Ltd

Wells, G. (1986) *The Meaning Makers*. London: Hodder and Stoughton

Wittgenstein, L. (1953) *Philosophical Investigations* Chichester: Blackwell

Zimmerman, B. (2000) *Self Efficacy: An Essential Motive to Learn*. Contemporary Educational Psychology 25 (1), 82 – 91

Index

Abboud, S K and Kim, J	142
age related norms	101, 150, 152, 155, 156
Antikainen, A	127
assessment	40, 60, 117, 129, 130, 132, 133, 136, 137
audio books	110
autonomous	25, 65, 130, 132, 176
Badman, G	25, 26
Bissex, G L	41
Blake N, Smeyers, P Smith, R and Standish, P	78, 184
Blunden, A	141
Britton, J	105
Brown, K	191
Browne, A	57, 158, 159, 162
Bruner, J	32, 142
Cilliers, P	188, 189, 198
Clark, M	23, 60, 106
cognitive skill	38, 75, 89, 183
Coles, G	157, 183, 186
Colman, A	184
community of practice	73, 75, 77, 90, 100
computers	22, 36, 44, 53, 59, 62, 73, 93, 105, 108, 110, 111, 113, 114, 172
curriculum	20, 31, 70, 74, 77, 87, 89, 138, 145
deficit theories	105, 116, 156
Deleuze G and Guattari, F	27
Department for Education	20, 38
De-schooling	170
Dhillon, A	105
Doman: *Teach Your Baby to Read*	52, 91
Dowty, T	31
Dr Seuss	54, 133, 180
dyslexia	165, 166, 167, 173

Education Otherwise	24
Elliot, R K	36
Ferreiro, E	89
Fischer, S R	21, 59
Fortune-Wood, M	30
Foucault, M	185
games	22, 28, 44, 52, 53, 59, 79, 80, 110, 111, 112, 113, 114, 115, 123, 153, 162, 172, 179
Gee, J P	114
Gibb, N	118
Gleick, J	187
Global Home Education Conference	30
Gorard, S	187
Goswami, U	156, 185
Graff, H J	15, 16, 17, 142
Gramley, S	49
Haggis, T	184, 185
Harris, R	49, 62
Harrison, A	12, 17, 118
Harry Potter	101, 119, 131, 138, 180
hidden curriculum	74
Holt, G	37
Home education numbers	26
Illich, I	170
Jesson, R McNaughton, S and Kolose, T	121
Kunzman, R	142
Lacqueur, T	11
Lakoff, G. and Johnson, M	36, 42
Lancy, D	82, 88, 90, 176
Lave, J and Wenger, E	39, 73, 75, 100
Learning curve	117
Downward	121
Incremental	125

Trajectories	28, 119, 120, 127, 180
Legitimate Peripheral Participation	73
Lewis, I M	34
literacy	14, 141, 142
emergent	74
minimum Standard	153
Long, E	141
look and say	21
McMillan, G. and Leslie, M	174
Meighan, R	30
memory	56, 57, 58, 71, 171, 172
metaphor	
acquisition	21, 37, 38, 39, 40, 75, 78, 89, 90, 108, 156, 184, 186, 193
Osmosis	192, 193
participation	30, 37, 38, 39, 42, 73, 74, 75, 99, 100, 108, 109, 114, 179, 186, 193
transmission	11, 88, 94, 95, 106, 111, 112, 141, 192, 195
Monk, D	142
Morrow, L M	148
National Literacy Trust	141
natural curiosity	94, 148, 179
Newton	187
Nicholson, F	30
Non-progressive learning	124
Olssen, M	161, 188
Open Systems	194
Oxford Reading System	117
Pattison, H	11, 19, 22, 26, 67, 73, 74, 114, 140, 153, 182, 191
Peim, N and Flint, K	10, 35
Penketh, C	169
Petrie, A Windrass, G & Thomas, A	26
phonemic awareness	117, 158, 184, 185, 186, 191
phonics	21, 26, 43, 44, 45, 46, 47, 48, 49, 50, 51, 52, 53, 54, 56, 61, 69, 79, 81, 87, 88, 108, 110, 115, 122, 143, 146, 155, 156, 157, 158, 162, 170, 186, 190
Pokemon	113, 114, 123

Popkewitz, T	63
positive non-interference	86
Post modernism	187
Prins, E and Toso, B W	20

reading
aloud	28, 59, 60, 61, 76, 77, 92, 95, 96, 97, 98, 99, 100, 101, 102, 104, 105, 110, 135, 159, 180, 184
Late	19, 21, 28, 81, 101, 118
Love of...	93, 94, 149
readiness	148, 149
schemes	21, 44, 54, 92, 121, 152, 165, 166, 198
silent	59, 61, 62
Reddy, M	36
Rogoff, B	39, 176
Rothermel, P	30

Saint Augustine of Hippo	43
School house	24
schooling	11, 12, 15, 20, 30, 64, 67, 73, 129, 141, 142, 169, 170, 172, 174, 183, 185, 196
self-organisation	182, 188, 189, 190, 191
Sfard, A	36, 37, 38, 39
Slavin, R Lake, C, Davis, S Madden, N	20, 138
Smith, F	39, 45, 49, 74
socio-cultural theories	186
Socratic dialogue	154
Special Educational Needs	28, 162, 169
Stainthorp R and Hughes D	20, 23, 56, 58, 61, 74
Stake, R E	27
Stanovich, K	183, 184
Steiner	87
structure	25
Suissa, J	30, 142, 145

symbolic
form	44, 45, 49, 63
representation	35
system	35
synthetic phonics	50

Taylor, M	9, 188, 193
teaching	
pre-empting	86
rejecting	22, 83, 88, 104, 150
self	85, 88
television	46, 110, 115, 116
Terzi, L	169
texting	114
Thomas, A	9, 13, 21, 22, 23, 26, 31, 41, 65, 67, 73, 74, 114, 153
Tintin	101
Tizard, B and Hughes, M	109
Torgeson, J	117
Toys	110
Trevarthen, C	79
Tsabar, B	82
UNESCO	89, 141
unschooling	92
US Department of Education	30
Usher, R and Edwards, R	197
Waldorf	70
Weinberger, J	74
Wells, G	67, 97, 105, 185
whole word approach	52, 156
Wittgenstein	35
World of Warcraft	59, 110, 113, 114, 178
Zimmerman, B	91

About the Author

Harriet Pattison has an academic background in social anthropology. Her own children were home educated, sparking a long term interest in learning to read which later became the subject of her PhD thesis. She continues to ponder and write on philosophies of literacy and alternative education and remains fascinated by the subject of learning. She is a lecturer in Early Childhood at Liverpool Hope University.